The Postmodern Temperaments:
Fifteen Poets

THE POSTMODERN TEMPERAMENTS: FIFTEEN POETS

Edited By
SANTOSH KUMAR

CYBERWIT.NET
2003

The Postmodern Temperaments: Fifteen Poets

FEATURING POEMS BY
Adam Gaucher
Alexander Shaumyan
Christine Kempster
Colette
Daniel W. Gonzales
Danielle Ackley-McPhail
Darla E. Fitzgerald
Del Senkbeil
Henry Victor
Herbert L. Burd
Janet I. Buck
John Dempsey
Kazuyosi Ikeda
Richard Conrad Henry
Serge van Duijnhoven

Published by
Cyberwit.net
4/2B, L.I.G. Govindpur Colony,
Allahabad-211004 (U.P.) India
Tel: 91-532-2541153
E-mail: cyberwit@rediffmail.com

Artwork by Colette

ISBN 81-901366-5-8
First Printing

Note: The Postmodern Temperaments: Fifteen Poets is a work of fiction and non-fiction. Characters, places, and incidents are created by the poet's imagination, and any resemblance to actual persons, living or dead, events, or locales is entirely coincidental.

Typeset by Vaishnavi Enterprises, 220/71-C/1, Kamla Nagar, Allahabad
Printed in India at Astha Associates, D. N. Marg, Allahabad

Qui si convien lasciare ogni sospetto
*Ogni viltà convien che qui sia morta.**
—Dante, ***Divina Commedia***

---

*Here must all distrust be left:
All cowardice must here be dead.
(The English version is from Dante, *The Divine Comedy*, Illustrated Modern Library, 1944, p. 22). -Ed.

PREFACE

There is no doubt that till 1950s Eliot's reputation as the greatest poet in America has been universally accepted, though William Carlos Williams (1883-1963) and Hart Crane (1899-1932) disagreed with Eliot's poetic technique and negativism in *The Waste Land*, which according to Williams was 'a great catastrophe', 'an atom bomb' that destroyed the roots of English poetry. The postmodern poets have been deplored as exhausted. Barth's essay 'The Literature of Exhaustion' (1967) revealed that there is nothing left for the contemporary author to inspire. Besides, the postmodernists are warned by Deconstructionism of Jacques Derrida, who pointed out that the printed page is not so important as the reader-response. This very well suggests the disappearance of the artist in the postmodern era, since the reader creates the poem he reads. This reminds us of the famous statement made by Roland Barthes (1915-80): 'The author is dead.' The reader alone creates the poem.

Unconventional style alone, as used by the poets inspired by Vorticism, Futurism and Cubism, is not enough to create great poetry. The poets included in *The Postmodern Temperaments* have in several poems employed traditional poetic technique, and yet succeeded in writing some of the greatest lines. Even Wallace Stevens (1879-1955) whom Yvor Winters compared with Shakespeare and Donald Davie described him as ' a poet to be mentioned in the same breath as Eliot and Yeats and Pound', employed the old poetic technique and traditional themes. The poets selected for *The Postmodern Temperaments* are able to give some of the best lines in contemporary world poetry, even though several of their poems, unlike Eliot and Pound, seem to be uninfluenced by the English Metaphysical poets, French symbolists and the Andre Breton's Surrealist manifesto (1924):

The poems aptly show that there are several ways to unearth the meanings and values.

Invent the sickness, trip over pain
relief. Itch ourselves with pills and
numb our senses. But that is not
humanity! That is not nature! That is
intelligence! Culture at its best.
Be selfish; join the war on death.

(Adam Gaucher, 'Ape Raper')

The rain falls blue above your wild eyes
my love
and I'm born again to wonder
if that sweet kiss
has made me whisper
upon your fair skin.

(Alexander Shaumyan, 'Deborah,
I Think You'll Understand...')

Birth and Death are certain
The in between bits are our choices
The universal clock never stops
We can't say wait a minute
"I want to get off"
Life's journey has a purpose.
A beginning and an end
So enjoy and embrace and live to the full
Because one day the reaper will catch us all!!!

(Christine Kempster, 'Time')

if there shall ever be
a shortage of water
i shall remedy the drought
with my tears

(Colette, ' Water Shortage')

Even death isn't thrilling anymore
it doesn't have the same finality it used to
it drags on and on like some petulant child
begging for candy until his mother breaks
his arm. I am hungry for the grotesque
and the beautiful and the dead. I want
my life to be a parade of surreal creatures
all vying for a spot on Insanity Roe.

(Daniel W. Gonzales, 'The Hours')

Fiery death
Rains from the sky
As captive souls descend
Colliding with the pillars
Of the World,
The pyre from which
The Phoenix must ascend
and Freedom withstand
Jealousy's vicious assault.

(Danielle Ackley-McPhail,
'The Fall of World Trade')

Create a sanctuary
in your mind. Reserve a room
only for silence. Close
the mental doors
to all prevailing thoughts.
Keep out the world of confusion.

(Darla Elaine Fitzgerald,
'Speak No Inner Dialogue')

Deep in my heart you planted a seed,
That memorable night, so long ago.
And from that tiny little seed,
A beautiful rose did grow.

(Del Senkbeil, 'Our Rose')

Jesus, I saw you hanging on the cross
Like a slaughtered goat for public sale
Condemned by the elders who induced the masses to 'crucify'
Convicted by Annas and Caiphas the diligent chief priests!

(Henry Victor, 'I Saw You Hanging')

What was the present is now the past.
What was the past is now the present.
People in this life have been such a trip.

(Herbert L. Burd, 'Screamin' Lisa')

Horns just blared in such impatient unison.
I wanted to scream, be the cradle of an angel,
make my loudness carry you
to safer places than this world.

(Janet I. Buck, 'Scar Tissue')

… Question: What're you going to do
when the brilliance doesn't come? When that one line, one word, one
anything doesn't come? Answer: The only thing that you can do.
Type something like this and wait.

(John Dempsey, '3 Am Waiting')

My heart is an iron nail, firm and straightforward.
The fine girl! I will attain my desire inward.
By driving the nail straightly, I will win the heart.
The nail, my heart, shall firmly pierce thee to the heart.

(Kazuyosi Ikeda, 'Sincere Love')

Death's beaconing
from different angles
Fear twitches my fingertips
as Silence approaches.

(Richard Conrad Henry, 'With Bated Breath')

this is the place where very soon
you will be one of those persons
missing, this is the place where
very soon you will be one of those
reported dead or disappeared

(Serge van Duijnhoven, 'Night In Hotel Orbit')

The variety of these poems is evident, and the fifteen authors succeed in writing poems full of grace and classic charm, even without indulging in 'parodies of middle ages'. Postmodernism according to Charles Jencks is 'disruption from within, refusing to submerge difference into universalism and therefore preserving multiplicity and local cultures' (*Postmodern Theory: The Current Debate*, 1992, ed. Patricia Waugh). *The Postmodern Temperaments* features the best work of the great masters of contemporary world poetry in English. The large number of selected poems by each poet contributes to a full revelation of the characteristic quality and main theme of these remarkable authors.

Cordially,
SANTOSH KUMAR

CONTENTS

- AT THE END OF THE DAY HE SITS IN THE SAME CHAIR EVERY TIME
- NAZBERRY SPACE FRUIT
- PIECE ONE WITH RESPECT TO THE EPIDEMIC
- ENTERTAINING A BOX OF FABRIC
- FOR WHAT? S
- THE YAWN MINUS FLEURS
- APE RAPER
- THE DESERTED FANFARE TREPANATION HORRAY!
- WITH LAUGHTER, GASPS AND HEART ATTACKS
- THE URGENT MESSAGE
- HE VACUUM TWENTY-THREE COCA COLA
- MINIMALISM
- ODD AND LOVELY OTHER PEOPLE
- LOU'S MODERN
- WHO INVENTED FEBRUARIES

By Adam Gaucher

AT THE END OF THE DAY HE SITS IN THE SAME CHAIR EVERY TIME

The older one that is, after the excitement of
every-second mundane existence, (unlike his
perception of the subject anyway); that's him by
the window in the small apartment building.

His preference is gin and coffee; a crude
mixture invented by the servants he wishes
he'd known and lost in a bad deal.
Behind him there's a dim light, provided by the
sort of thing that would likely frequent a downtown
main avenue pizza dive. It gives the
kind of splash that the atmosphere is just thirsting
for, and he knows what that's all about; and
he knows it's no mistake.

He lights a cigarette due by six minutes past.
The rain is a distraction because it is so
beautiful, and he wouldn't mind the chance to
dance around out there. That's what he
writes about (dancing in the rain, for real),
but he's not happy with it.
It's not his style. He places it in
the pile of future drawing paper, which he
never gets around to, but is nice
to know is there for him should he need it.

He presents himself a fresh leaf. Some
time passes. Tonight doesn't appear to be
his; he's hardly getting it rolling. Soon enough
there's a pleasant knocking at the door.
The usual friend floats in content and sexed,

sits at the usual couch and starts in with the
usual banter. It's over. For a spell what his
friend is boasting doesn't register in his head,
but eventually he accepts the circumstances.
Instead of accusing this friend of robbing him
of a great poem, he figures he's just rescued
him from the worst one.

NAZBERRY SPACE FRUIT

Charlie bent the juicy Lucy; the captain of
the ship; married forty eight people off the
eastern shore, and drowned them all slowly,
two by two. Consequently the moon penetrated
blushing secrets in the sand, including Mozart's
failing heartbeat, and the beauty of disease.

Life on Mars was David winking. He grew
up on a branch with a vine in his belly.
Nearly twenty five of them refused the usual
orbit and ended up here. Some tell stories
of explosions and repair, while most hide in
style under the Chapeaux Mossant.

The age of Space Fruit fell us the twins and
his brother, the planet queen Janis, and
another poet just to be blunt about it.
There wasn't enough time to hand it out like
Tuesday's exclusive sale on slavery. These
fantastic creatures had cratered the Earth
securing their graves, pleasantly obsessed with
the tombstone blues.

Coda: The rarity of specific insects, including
two steps behind them their obtuse
predators following, was a sick excuse for
justice, and was in the poorest of taste. The
headlines produced the alternative outlook
(two queers for inspiration, etc.), and that
stupidity was believed most because it
was made simple to match their minds.

PIECE ONE WITH RESPECT TO THE EPIDEMIC

One of the more potentially ugly parts of the
human male body is the section peeking
just over the collar where the back of
the neck meets the back of the head.
This would be more accurately refered to as the nape.
Two things are usually required from the subject
to make this site completely ugly. First,
he must have had his head shaved, or simply
have become naturally hairless. Second, he must be
slightly overweight, or muscular enough to have
converted this usually somewhat attractive area
into an almost completely flat surface of
dumb repulsive flesh. Of course there are instances where
the back of one's head does not protrude out as much
as any other's might, where the individual would
not necessarily have to meet the
criteria in full to sport an ugly nape.

In Reynold's postulate of 1976,
Reynold suggests that the gradual size increase
of shirt collars in popular fashion, and
the ever-growing population of young males with
long hair, are in direct correlation with
a sudden outbreak of ugly napes. He
continues by laying out a course of action
which he believes will solve the problem.
This action involves pushing the insecurity of not
being rich, rather than the usual insecurity push
of not being attractive. Reynold's ingenious
plan places the burden of this task upon
the well established mass media. Camera
shots of ugly napes belonging to young males

with money and women would certainly be
utilized to their fullest. Expensive wines, cars and business suits
would be the new medium of sexual attraction,
as opposed to, and outdating the current yet still
atrocious medium of external aesthetics.

ENTERTAINING A BOX OF FABRIC

There are often people who'll rub
their eyes from beneath their glasses
as if it were some photographer's sick
fetish for heroin, blood and fucking.
What's worse are the artists who'll
tell you it's not wise to call them at work;
their excuse being "suffocation." (Most
likely from the noir beyond it).

And some people's illustrators; hanging
themselves on some obscure public wall.
It's clear and sad, but everyone knows they
could have made a better pair of shoes.
That's where most of the money goes anyway:
a good blank stare, or trimmed hedges as if
the sake of the neighborhood's morale was
on the table.

The poet's dress size is a flesh-coloured
bikini. Not unlike posing nude in the
first place for your family's palette, (the
parents and the parents' parents, etcetera).
Some days, like a phenomenon, creation is
only practiced. In the studio directors try
to figure it all out: Fade in. Thank you horny
insects that it's finally over. They missed it.
Pan away.

FOR WHAT?S

This is where I'll lose it:
Allow the clevers to dissect my
being and become the fading shadow
of my former self. No longer will
negative six be a pleasure to me.
I will find the clothes that'll bring
the most notice, and I'll wear them.

I'll believe it's seventy three. I'll
be waiting for the fifth album, still.
I'll tell stories for the next generation
of horrible poets to admire. They'll be
gathered for a fix of decrepit senile
genius, but I'll be too busy taking
pictures of the seventh world war.

I'll smoke too much and drink not
enough. I'll settle for cinnamon when
there isn't any honey. My books will
rape me, and convince me that I
wasn't worth a damn. And I'll finally
accept my belief that four is the
perfect number of stanzas in a poem.

THE YAWN MINUS FLEURS

The frame; (is) destined to be a
yawn minus fleurs, or at its best a flavour
minus kissing. Through a presence
which recoils lying somber, is that
stupid reunion between unknowing fortunates.
(Sort of a red flag here for the locals).

"Keep 'em coming!" screams precious
princess bristles. Everyday the same
thing, another breakdown. Eat a
breadstick and drink it black. Get
your hair cut, and wipe your nose.
Nowhere to turn right? Isn't that
what the child was singing?

City population sign flies a kite
in his underwear at two in the morning.
Isn't that what the evening's meal
was singing? "Now I just want a
cigarette," responds a poet, in full
colour and all, and that whole scene.
The losers stumble out of thought,
as all normal people wear silk pajamas.

One should stop soon. It's
become pointless, and immeasurable. Almost
perfect. Its fingernails are too sharp
for a ghost to scratch its head
without learning to laugh in the
process. Someone must seem to know
what it all comes down to, but maybe
not quite, or quiet, or quit.

APE RAPER

Inside the skull. The skull and what's
inside it. Clearly enough to boast,
or at least boast with anyway. Such
organization we've produced: a system,
a limitation. We are the discarded jokers
when (even) playing solitaire; the special
untainted variety of living dust and
meat.

Invent the sickness, trip over pain
relief. Itch ourselves with pills and
numb our senses. But that is not
humanity! That is not nature! That is
intelligence! Culture at its best.
Be selfish; join the war on death.

Give me tickets tickets tickets! I've
broken father law at my very fault:
I was born into poverty! O Lord
won't they shorten my chain for
what I have done! I love my
country and I hate the other high
school. I will burn the flags of
all inferior nations!

Satire? Smells like it. One of
those inventions they weren't sure of
how to use so they gave it to
the poets. Hey, look where the
penis fits! And the moral of the story:
Stupidity lies in thinking we're intelligent.
Intelligence lies in knowing that we are
stupid. (Like this poem).

THE DESERTED FANFARE TREPANATION HORRAY!

Her face he must have seen before,
as practically magazine as it was.
He bought the subscription he thought
would last a life time, he performed
a double take, then realized it was me.

"Adam," he spoke aloud, "I almost fell in
love with you, but I'm still willing to
father your child." With these magic words
I leapt from the page and stated,
"My children have already been born
grown and gone, it would torment
them to have another invisible sister."

The look on his face only placed third
in the photo finish. I took second,
and first had been awarded to the
book seller near Center Street. Later
we all had coffee and laughed over
good times until the Paparazzi caught
me staring at the breasts of the
waitress' awaiting paycheck.

With that magic action I lingered
slowly back into the pages where I
belonged. "Adam," he spoke aloud, "you
lived a good life, but you were even
better in bed (so I've been told)."
"It's true," were my last words, "I did sleep
well, and I never was known to snore."

He realized that one's brain never
develops until it learns how to
stop thinking, but he ran out of
money soon after and couldn't afford
the next issue. He never did read
the proper ending.

WITH LAUGHTER, GASPS AND HEART ATTACKS

I look about the emptiness. A couple
stumbles in, adding to the emptiness. I
talk about the atmosphere to my little piece
of paper, then add it to the emptiness. So
the fallen cutlery speaks in Morse code,
"Save the ship! Let the damned children swim!"

As always the ruckus is overem-
bellished by entertainment poachers
with laughter gasps and heart attacks.
The fat man chokes. Beady
eyes bleed for social understanding.
I feel like being hung from trees then
eaten by commercial artists from the
later half of nineteen eighty six.

Some friends come and some friends
go. Most friends like to
vomit on you. I escape in a
cigarette like the poor slob who
collects brown paper sacs from liquor
stores to win the queen mother's sympathy.
"There are none taxed in
Greenwich Village," speaks a purple
heart, "you know you're killing yourself,
don't you?"

I look about the ugliness. A couple
stumbles out, adding to the beauty. It
is another empty night out with me (the
one hardly in reserve to warm the benches),
and it's time for the next pot of coffee.

This is the best. Better than anything
less or more. Mediocrity is key, as
I watch the headlights pass away in the
rain like capsized sarcophagi built for two.

THE URGENT MESSAGE

A message floated lonely to my
tiny island. It did look urgent, but
I was busy. Selfishly, I tossed it
on the dresser and went out to
paint the town various shades of
orange and red. Half way through
the tide came in, and I couldn't
help worrying about the French
lego castle that I was building so
that I'd never be defeated by the
Spanish and English armies. My
friends thought I was crazy, but it
sure was a grand structure, wasn't it?

HE VACUUM TWENTY-THREE COCA COLA

Realize, it's quite cold today
for the choosy human being.
"This ain't Miami beach sister!"
I agree geographically.

You're one of those people who
don't eat the peels off of oranges
aren't you? "Why actually, yes
I am!" Well, you'll not find me in
that euphoric pancake morning
anytime soon. Continue painting.

(Turn to reader, proceed slow walk).

I've found that the difference between
an artist and a good artist is
that the good artist actually knows they
produce nothing but crap. Then
there are the great artists who don't
produce anything at all, usually in
acting, every second of their lives.
Because it's one for the honey. Two
for the blow. Three for stuffed
Betty on Thanksgiving day, and
goat bleat goat.

What you've seen here is how
we have generated a prime example
of crap-core artistics. (The big
breasted super model situates her
arms to further aid in advertising
the aforementioned product. She

also sports a mini skirt). You'll
find when reading that the cerebral
cortex is not genuinely pleased
throughout with this outcome.
Observe again:
I thank you for wasting your
time and mine.

Last call!
Fade out: a varied clink of glass
and the unintelligible conversing
of a small crowd.

MINIMALISM

A poem flew in and flew around.
My imagination tried to kill.
It hung there above the tobacco
burning, and sailed silent through
bellows underneath high cheek
bones. A poem flew in and landed
on my page. Here it sits now for
me to be proud of.

ODD AND LOVELY OTHER PEOPLE

Fascination occurred blindly upon fear's
destination of acceptance complete with
history's petty lessons throughout. (The
whore's hair was also combed gently
northward by that evening's wind). In
order for the feature presentation to begin,
twenty three culture jamming coca-comas
were sold out at regular price. In
short morbid royalties shared together
these favors.

And then they gathered.

The odd and lovely other people are not
she which walks so pathetically filtered.
Nor is he who's lower part of the
leg telescopes into the upper part of the
leg. Too often one case of mis-
taken identity leads us to yet another
exponential uprising of ribbon cutting
ceremonies surrounding the individual at
hand. Truth is expelled from the lusting
judges where a critic's wish breaks
nowhere but even. So said he,
"I've once loved a Trojan's failure."

And then they wept.

With joy squaring off against drooling
folk and fiends seen is our refusal
to ban expressions on these faces.
In that we charm less, but it is the

least which deems charming. Correct
me if I should ever be so wrong mon
frÃ¨re. Please leave your two quarters
and pay up front. (This is no ultimate
cause for misshapen playground!)

LOU'S MODERN

Every day I wake up not realizing
why I think these people are so
wonderful. I usually stand drooling
the night's dreams at this point
against porcelain in serenity until the
piss hits the pool and I'm deaf
beyond heartbreak. And so I walk
downtown amongst the patterned
sadness, straddled on a pilgrimage
to find faces willing to invent new
things. Failed, slumping into the
usual poetic destination, the slaves
curtsy and place my sorry ass into
the more drab of corners. There
I sit with best friends the cup and
pen. They say I'm content with
my surroundings and am fabulous
anyway. I'd generally agree with
them, if it weren't for just that.

WHO INVENTED FEBRUARIES

A bearded Japanese wise man (because
all wise men are bearded Japanese) once
said he wished he could have seen how
beautiful that girl really was in order to
know how worthy she'd been of grabbing
that much of his attention. He'd also been
searching for "a girl who's hair was so fair
it could floss the daemons out of one's
teeth" for quite some time now. One of
those medieval quests I guess; nothing I've
ever found to be too worthwhile. My
bag's always been in the asterisks for the
blind to know where I've last left my
shuffled thoughts. "My love is knowing
the colour of your eyes," and such jazz, like
Father Nonsense flashing peace in northern
Georgia (though you shouldn't trust him
with your last two slices of bread).

Unfortunately this whole ordeal's presence
in Ireland was ill met and had been forced
to pay homage to the locals' d-minor
favoritism. Survival was tops, but at first
stumbled loosely in the jungles. I (who was
back home surrounded by various apes,
berries and roaming ponies) suddenly
realized that there was a boat to be caught.
But that was well over five years gone at
this point , so I triangulated the fellowship's
position and fell asleep.

I awoke to the sounds of selfish high heels
and to the gag reflex of an underaged
alcoholic in the Past Radicals' Showroom.
I told the girl there (who was nailing my feet
to the wall when they could have just tied
my hands behind me and hung me by my
armpits) that she needed to find my friend
the bearded Japanese wise man (because
all wise men are bearded Japanese) who
was hanging out with Father Nonsense and
the rest by now, according to my calculations,
somewhere out on the edges of space. She'd
seen at that moment why I was to be nailed
to a wall and stole my pocket calender which
I had circled and highlighted. Explanations
for the important dates were printed neatly
in the index.

By Alexander Shaumyan

PLACE WHERE LIGHT IS

In these cold rainy nights,
In these streets, in these dreams
I'll walk in my solitude
To a place where light is.

Do not ask who I am,
Do not ask where I go—
I've lost all direction,
Yet I always knew this—
I'll find my way back
To a place where light is.

No, it can't be that far—
I've walked many miles,
I've seen it in a smile
Of a girl like a breeze—
I'll find my way back
To a place where light is.

I've been walking in darkness
Of frozen minds,
I saw hearts that were numb
And eyes that were blind,
I saw tears and pain,
War and disease,
But I just kept on walking
To a place where light is.

Yes, I know it's near,
By those mulberry trees
And those valleys of daffodils,
Where the hummingbirds sing,

Where my love rests in waiting
With a smile like a breeze—
Yes, I'll find my way back
To a place where light is.

KENTUCKY GIRL

(for Christy)

Yes, you are, yes, you are, my love,
You're my lovely Kentucky girl.

In your bourbon smile I can see
Grassy hills just as free as you—
Come, my darling, won't you sit with me—
We'll have a beer or two.

In that hair that shines like the sun,
Freckled skin and untamed, sparkling eyes
I can see the Kentucky sky
And the valleys where the horses run wild.

I remember when I was a child
And the wind would embrace my face,
I'd smile like you smile tonight,
Thinking this is the time and place.

As I stand here at a local saloon,
The same child is awake in me—
Struck by love in the Kentucky moon—
Thinking this is where I'd like to be.

And the moon seems to sign your name
In your eyes that sparkle like pearls—
Yes, you are, yes, you are, my love,
You're my lovely Kentucky girl.

RAPE OF A POET

"If lust and hate is the candy,
if blood and love taste so sweet,
then we give 'em what they want."
—Natalie Merchant, 10,000 Maniacs

How quickly idols fall—here's the one
That's selling truth and sneakers,
Here's another selling underwear,
Justice, peace, and beer—
Their revolution's dead, there's only fear
Of dark obscurity, of not being a star—
Their fans are blind, their eyes are fixed
On something that's intangible and far—
Yes, yes, they need that perfect ass and car,
Those biceps and those sacred breasts
That magazines and factories caress
Like engineered parts—
Here's your leg, my head, your jaw, my heart,
That's pulverized in dirt,
We're making love like faucets
In the dark
With mouthwashed movements
And mechanical embraces—
Here's the one that's selling love
And hackneyed lines— "I love you, baby,
Yes, tonight it's real"—
Here's a nose job and plastic smiling faces,
A blow job, a hand job and a jolt
Inside my head, my head that bursts like atom
And farts throughout Universe like Big Bang
Inside some Einstein figure made of wax,

Yes, here's your Washington, here's your Lincoln,
Your Malcolm X, your Martin Luther King,
Here's your Elvis, Jesus and Sid Vicious,
Here's your dead rich uncle Phil or Bill
Or Duckbilled Platypus,
Here's your supermodel, your vibrator,
Your lubricated condom and your tax,
Here's your lyric poet, raped and violated—
Spread-eagled on a page like some cheap whore,
While you keep shouting "MORE" and "MORE" and "MORE"...

WHY JOHNNY CAN'T DO MATH

He likes to watch a porno in his room,
Rewind the tape to see the close-up shots,
"My God! She does them both—what a slut!"
He thinks. Perhaps the stars, the moon

Could be romantic. But that's what Johnny likes—
He likes to watch a porno in his room,
He likes the lights, the camera that zooms
In on the action. While inside

Something's not right, something's rotten here—
It's not that he can't read. The books
He opens occasionally and burps and looks
At how he does her, and she does him. And beer

Tastes very good and very nice indeed.
The girls say: "Johnny, you're not a queer."
And Johnny likes his pornos and his beer,
And that is all that Johnny really needs.

HEY MR. DEATH

Hey Mr. Death,
My old and fated friend,
I greet you with a welcoming denial,
I felt you once before, your frosted breath
And your dark face at many murder trials
That followed countless victims to their end.

Hey Mr. Death,
When love is such that we
Yield to a sudden urge to kill our mate,
When you can turn around and find hate
Inside the eyes of someone next to you,
When wealth's to be enjoyed but by a few,
Who wouldn't give you anything for free,
You come, my friend, and take it all away.

Hey Mr. Death,
I laugh as if I fall
Into the graveyard of the living dead,
Where the insurance clerks have made their bed
With sickness covers and malpractice sheets
That cushion every blow that you deal,
Yet deep inside I know, I can feel
My heart that's pounding, with every beat
It's getting closer to your final call.

Hey Mr. Death,
I want to say good-bye
To those who somehow have been wronged,
I've heard their death throes, their final cries
That rose like a question mark in pain,
But there's no answer, what remains
Is life without answers and sad songs.

DEBORAH, I THINK YOU'LL UNDERSTAND...

Deborah,
I think you'll understand what I mean
when at night I sleep on the surfaces of books
and dream of paper attics
Through the green mesh of your eyes
I see rooftops of innocence
and hills of joy

O how brilliant you are in the milky moon
O how tender is your walk through my eardrums

I collapse in my drunkenness
and watch the skies of wonder, O Deborah
I kiss the thin fabric of your lips
and journey through your hair

I'm lost, my love, in your negligee
of white horses and silky winds
Teach me the arithmetic of who you are
for I cannot add nor subtract your splendor

The rain falls blue above your wild eyes
my love
and I'm born again to wonder
if that sweet kiss
has made me whisper
upon your fair skin.

OUR SELVES, OUR GRAVES

"We are the hollow men
We are the stuffed men
Leaning together
Headpiece filled with straw."
—T.S. Eliot

Our graves will not be marked
by any memories of
What we've done, but
rather

We are our graves.
We step like phantoms
among walls of

Houses, inhaling loneliness.

Our graves will not be marked
by any trace or
sign of

Life. Lifeless is what we are,
our gaze is empty,
our breath is meaningless.

Our graves will not be marked
by stars or dreams,
Only cold comfort of tile
and glass, of clocks
and instruments.

Our graves, like our selves,
are covered
By masks and monuments
that scream for

Love, love buried deep inside

Our selves, our graves.

TOUCH

"Everything here is yellow and green."
—Anne Sexton

You pull me into your
delicate sea,
As I shiver at your touch,
Now I'm a valley and you're
a mountain,
Now I'm dark green and you're
bright yellow,
You play me like an instrument,
pulling my strings
one by one,
As I respond in a symphony
of poetic madness,
Crying on my pillow, I hug
the empty space
between us,
Longing for the night when
I first touched you.

Love, darling, is a silent mistress,
who comes streaming through
my fingers in gentle tears.
We have lost the softness
and the tenderness of her touch,
Sleeping on a bed of nails,
we scream in agony of her
passing.

But I know that deep inside you
there is a flower growing,
longing for the moisture
of a kiss, for the freedom
of the ocean.

We meet and part in its darkness,
leaving a trail of tears behind us.

A GIFT

Darling, I know it's hard see
And those voices tell you there is no use—
But, darling, listen, listen to me—
Those voices you hear—they lie to you.

For I am here, here for you
With my heart open wide to ease your pain—
And those voices, those demons are nothing new—
Their strength gets weaker with each new day.

Just raise the curtains and see the stars
And let my love lift you up tonight,
And let my music gently heal these scars,
As you rest in my arms till the morning light.

I know, darling, of these demons within,
That drag you down and pull you inside,
That mock you and tease you, that speak of sin,
But they aren't real—these demons are lies.

For you're beautiful, pure and strong—
Yes, you're stronger than any of them,
Just listen, darling, to my love's new song—
It shines inside me like a priceless gem.

When I was born, I always knew
There's more to this life than meets the eye
So I send this gift of my love for you
To set you free, like this moon in the sky.

A HARP PLAYER

I can remember the time
when I was young
and full of strange ideas,
I would dream a young girl,
who played
a golden harp on the ocean
rocks,
her little hands like gentle
bird feathers,
barely touching the strings,
as the sunlight played
upon her hair,
and her eyes always posed
a question—
Can you see him?
In these ocean depths
I lost my lover—
he was much like you,
foolish yet noble,
restless and
always ready for change.
Then she would disappear,
as I walked along the shoreline,
wondering who she was,
but somehow I knew
that she was my destiny...
And now each time I walk along
this shoreline,
I can hear her music and I know
that it was always me down there
at the bottom—
waiting for you, my love,
to draw me
out.

THE UNFINISHED PORTRAIT

(for Debbie)

The unfinished portrait is love.
Every day I try to finish it but never
seem to capture her beauty and purity,
a stroke here and there, but she always
looks more beautiful.

The unfinished portrait is love.
Every day I come to look at it and admire it,
her face has always captured my imagination,
yet there are still many pieces missing
and I cannot put it together.

She is much too beautiful to the eye.

The unfinished portrait is love.
Every day I come in tears to have a brief
glimpse of an imperfect likeness, finally
I gave it up, I will no longer try to
paint her.

But I picked up the brush once more and
began to paint.

The unfinished portrait is love.
You will not find her in the paintings
of da Vinci, Botticelli or Michelangelo.
She is never finished, but always there.
Never complete, yet always whole.

Like Van Gogh without an ear,
the unfinished portrait is love.

TO ANNE SEXTON

I am a dried-up leaf
that has fallen off the tree
of humanity.
It's autumn and we are all
falling one by one,
the green is lost to us
and we are all different
in color.

"We are of little faith," I hear
your voice in the wind.
Yes, we are of little faith.

A child has no weapons,
it is thrown empty-handed
into the world.

But now we all need protection.

Once we used sticks and stones
to protect what was ours,
but what was once ours is
no more, the tree is lost to us—
there is no security...

only death.

WITH YEARS

"With years your drive goes down,"
Said Dick the bartender,
Fixing another gin and tonic—
It made me think
Of you, my darling, so young and tender—
Another memory, another drink,
Another tip, another moment squandered
On platitudes and unsolicited advice,
Unheeded by my gypsy heart that wanders
Along these lonely streets as years go by.

With years your drive goes down
And your soul
Becomes accustomed to the daily grind—
With years you, too, become a local clown
Indifferent to everything and blind.

With years your drive goes down
And it's over—
Perhaps you marry or get happily divorced—
Whether you sleep alone or with someone,
You still can't tell what's better or what's worse.

With years your drive goes down
Is all I know—
Perhaps my love for you was but a dream,
But I'll have another drink before I go
Into the darkness with the final scream.

APOCALYPTIC DREAM

"Vanity of vanities, saith the Preacher,
vanity of vanities; all is vanity."
Ecclesiastes 1:2

A giant phallus rose in the sky,
I knew not how, still I wondered why
Until I heard the rabbi tell the priest
It was a sign that Someone's getting pissed.
I thought I heard it once on CNN
That men were sheep that only looked like men
Until my doubts finally dispersed,
I saw a phallus in the heavens burst—
A giant wiener with the balls aflame
That put my tiny private parts to shame—
Even Geraldo, Oprah, Larry King
Could not make sense of this humongous thing
That's bigger than O.J. and Princess Di,
It even made the nonbelievers cry...
And I cried out: "Twinkle from afar,
O giant Horn of Heaven, how huge you are,
Bringing great terror to the bravest men—
Is this the Judgment Day? Is this the End?"
And then the lightning flashed and thunder struck,
I heard the Major tell the Captain: "Duck!"
They ran for cover but it was too late,
The mighty wiener didn't hesitate
And struck its blows, going up and down again,
Crushing America, Russia, Japan,
China and India, Middle East, Brazil,
Reducing all the continents to nil...
And then the dust has settled in my eyes,
I woke up and soon I realized
The vanity of all the things I see
And felt alive again and truly free.

PERIOD DOUBLING ROUTE TO CHAOS

It starts somewhere at x and moves to y,
Zigzagging like a random fleeting z,
While in my heart it seems to multiply
And run away toward infinity.
It starts like some equation in a dream
That sums up all the things I feel in me—
This sky, this night, this moon—all somehow seem
To resonate in perfect symmetry.
This nightclub, where I come to spend my time
And contemplate the female form disrobed
Before the cheering throng of horny guys,
Where I still find a certain glimpse of hope—
A random spark that fuels my fantasy...
And when it's over, all the drunks return
To their dull and unfulfilling lives,
Yet in my mind and heart it twists and turns—
That random switch that's keeping me alive.

By Christine Kempster

THE THREE GRACES

Father in heaven no need to see him
Almighty on his throne
Invincible and omnipotent
Taken on trust no need to touch
Heaven waits for us all

Hope for the future
Optimism and faith
Prayers in the candles
Elevate the dream

Charity begins at home
Hope springs eternal
Alms for the needy
Reason never fails
Invention from necessity
Trust in humanity
Yes faith, hope and charity

TIME

Time and plenty of it
Time for this and that
But when it runs out
Its time to find
Heavens gates, or hell's fires
Which will it be for you and me
An eternity of heavenly pursuits
Or everlasting fire stoking
There's always the possibility some might say
That we come back for another try
What will we be this time I wonder
A cow or a tree, elephant or mouse
Another baby whose Mum says
'This ones been here before!'
Whatever the outcome
Time and tide wait for no one, they keep flowing
Leaving some of us behind like driftwood
Whilst carrying others along on the crests
Birth and Death are certain
The in between bits are our choices
The universal clock never stops
We can't say wait a minute
"I want to get off"
Life's journey has a purpose
A beginning and an end
So enjoy and embrace and live to the full
Because one day the reaper will catch us all!!!

FRIENDS AND RELATIONS

Choose your friends carefully
Spend days with them cheerfully
Friends can be wonderful
Yet they are rarely hateful

Relatives come with birth
Mum's and Dad's for all they're worth
Aunts and Uncles on the side
Grandparents we must abide

Brothers against sisters
Will never be the cats whiskers
But the pals we make a school
Are always hep and cool

Why then are we never happy
With the 'little chappie'
The weird family member
We'd like not to remember

Auntie Maud smelling of moth balls
Uncle Nige kicking the baby's ball
Grandpa Joe sleeps in a chair
While Grandma Flo is sadly lacking hair

All in all we'd like to forget
That family ties cannot be forgot
But friendships formed anew
Rarely go askew

BROUGHT INTO THE FOLD

Four little cherubs stand in a line
Four little heads do incline
Shower them with water
And sign them with the cross

Now they are baptised
They won't be ostracised
Because the family of Christ
Embraces the newborn Christian

Reborn into the church of Christ
For the young and old alike
Let faith blossom and bloom
For the Spirit wakens our love

THE LONG WAIT

Its gone seven
Should be in heaven
Still waiting for the bus
Lets not make a fuss

Why do we wait
Standing by the gate
Lets not make a fuss
Waiting for the bus

Looking out the window
Arms and legs akimbo
Waiting for the bus
Lets not make a fuss

Just behind the door
Resting on the floor
Lets not make a fuss
Waiting for the bus

WONDERFUL THINGS

Wisdom is a wonderful thing
You couldn't contemplate a fling
Seriousness is the order of the day
Sensibility guides your way

Spice up your life
Even get a wife
Maybe a child or two
Not too many, just a few

Don't live life dutifully
Make it through joyfully
Sing the days praises
Smile at the yellow daisies

Life is too precious
To be always anxious
Life is a wonderful thing
Make sure you do have a FLING

BO?

I must have BO
Can't be anything I said
I cleaned my teeth just yesterday
It must be BO

I've watched them leave
On their ownsome
Or two at a time
I've seen them leave

Almost alone now
I watch and wait
For the last one to go
Nearly alone now

There goes another
Three together this time
And only two left
Sorry there goes another

I must have BO
The last one has left
And I am bereft
It must be BO

No surely not
Only the customers have gone
Now the workers come out to play
It definitely was not!!

OH!

Oh! You are adorable
And nothing but trouble
Playing there in the rubble

Oh! You are a trial
But I would walk a mile
For you and your cheeky smile

Oh! You are a lucky lad
Loved by your old dad
Even when you make him mad

Oh! You are a quiet lump
Now the day is over at the dump
And you are looking soft and damp

Oh! You are a cherub
Nice and clean from the tub
Now to bed my little grub

Oh! You little dove
Sleep now under the moon above
And Mummy will watch over you with her love

THE SHAMEFUL HUSSEY

The shameful hussey
Was always fussy
Her naughty knickers
Meant to raise sniggers

She hangs them on the line
For Freddie at number nine
Giving him the sign
To make sure he'd be on time

She is so fussy
The shameful hussey
Raising little titters
With her naughty knickers

ROGER

Roger the lodger
Was never a bodger
Came to stay
And wouldn't go away

Best man at the wedding
Brought his own bedding
Then came roaring
On his motorbike soaring

He really is a lovely man
Even when he brought the dustpan
Shame he couldn't stay
When we showed him the way
TO GO HOME !!!

THEY'VE NICKED ME ONLY THOUGHT

They've nicked me bike
They've nicked the Pink Panther
They've nicked me transport
They've nicked me only thought…!

I shall have to walk
I'll have to use the train
I'll have to ride a bus
They've nicked me only thought…!

How can I tell me friends
How will I tell the insurance
How can I admit
They've nicked me only thought…!

Gutted I am
Sick inside with loss
Ashamed after all these years
They've nicked me only thought…!

Whoever they are
Whatever they are
Cruel slugs though they be
They've nicked me only thought…!

I can only wait for
The coppers at me door
And a statement I shall make
They've nicked me only thought…!

THE STOCKS AT NIGHT

Sitting all alone
Can't lay down
Waiting for what
Covered in grot

Feet and hands
Slotted in holes
Chained and raw
Can't sleep, won't sleep

Dawn has broken with
No rest at all
He's still there
But waiting for what

What's so wrong
That he's still there
How bad could he be
That he's still there

Took a loaf
To feed seven empty bellies
Seven little bodies
In need of food

He'll be off to Oz
Said the beak
And soon seven little bodies
Won't need any food

TWO LITTLE GIRLS

Two little girls
Pretty as can be
Looking like their mummy
And good as good can be
Loved by Nanny and Pop
Mummy and Daddy too
Two little girls
Pretty as can be

MONDAY TO SUNDAY

Monday begins the week
It's the day between rest and hard work

Tuesday begins the grind
Too early in the week too much still ahead

Wednesday and we're half way there
Looking back, looking forward

Thursday and the weekend is creeping closer
Most of the slog is over

Friday just one more day
So work today for all you're worth

Saturday – up early to rave all day
Evening comes the raving doesn't stop

Sunday is the one day of rest
Because come the morning it'll be MONDAY and work!

CHANGE

Change I will he says
Pigs might fly say I

Mature I will he says
In a month of Monday's say I

Get my life together he says
Yeh! Yeh! Say I

I'm a pussy cat he says
But the tiger I see say I

I'm a good boy mum he says
I'll believe you one day say I

- **AMOUR VICTORIEUX**
- **ENDURING FREEDOM**
- **WATER SHORTAGE**
- **WILD CAGE**
- **PARADISE LOST**
- **HOPELESS SHAPELESS THUNDER**
- **IT'S HUMAN NATURE**
- **FRESH WATER MIRAGE**
- **THE SENSES**
- **BIRD OF PARADISE**
- **CURE FOR (SELF) HATRED**
- **STIGMATA**
- **SOMETIMES**
- **LOVE IS A FABLE**
- **CIRQUE DE COLETTE**

By Colette

AMOUR VICTORIEUX

there was a hand
on my head
forcing me beneath the sea
attempting to drown
my dreams of love, and
aspirations of artistry

i swallowed the salt water
fought for air
swam with sharks
i was Mother Nature's child
seeking prayer

there was a myth
so it's been written, so it's been told
in the many books under one binding
inked by human drones, and
read by many more
that women are the subservient sex

i lingered in their purgatory
bit the fist of my suppressor
to rise again, walk on water
and greet *you*
the devil's successor

there was a nymph
the winged goddess of victory
who alighted on my soul's prow
she was my guide, a thunderbolt yours
to the lighthouse—our meeting ground
the future—our blissful promise

ENDURING FREEDOM

there's a breath in the air
that blew in with perfection's breeze
i've invited it
my opportunity to seize

a woman of the Amazon
slayer of cynicism
your warrior princess
impregnated with hope
a temple with a dress
the safe haven
where dreams are confessed

freedom
is the purity of life beyond our own
my father, brother, you
the strength, which crumbles stones

there's a breath in the air
close your eyes and inhale
i'll anoint you with raindrops
fear subsiding, love will prevail

the state of our union
misunderstood battles
none ignited by our fuel
fencing with steak knives
an unlikely duel
adversity our challenge
braveness our tool

heavenly peace
is to be found by those who seek
believe in this sweet victory
the inheritors of our earth shall not be meek

there's a breath in the air
belonging to you, a necklace of kisses
embracing your honor
deserving of my wishes

WATER SHORTAGE

if there shall ever be
a shortage of water
i shall remedy the drought
with my tears

swallowed
by the whale of love
call me Jonah
and i'll cry
a sea of fears

the years
get misplaced
the scars
still visible
like a manatee
i'm endangered
not invisible

barely livable
my environment
barren of true love
i scream for help
echoes fall
only on deaf ears

i talk to God
no one answers
drowning
in my sorrows
i wonder
if she hears

WILD CAGE

my doe eyes   invited you
your body   accepted
words   fragrant as lilacs
emanating   from your lips

i followed   the false scent
without knowledge   without facts

accepting you   welcoming you
into my garden   my forest
i   raising butterflies
you   sowing oats
full-bodied   grape vines
any stag   would drink
you kneeled   in genuflection
i bowed   in servility

naive   little fawn
what i am   i think

emotionally nude   psychologically crippled
you hovered   clouds covered
i strained   to view sunshine
through fog   through rain
fight   you choose
i choose   flee
a hunter's sacrifice   i won't be

unhitch   your dirty trap
empty it   not me

PARADISE LOST

a virgin mistress
precarious in type, created
in the unbearable likeness
of you

a glowing nimbus
heart on canvas, dripping
from the rough edges
of life

a keyboard's pen
whisperer of promises, screaming
for the quiet reciprocation
of love

a surrogate violin
empathy in melodies, singing
to the bandaged soul
of hope

a babbling brook
moonlight on mystery, dancing
around the enchanted spirit
of dreams

a cupid's psyche
acquirer of wings, captured
in the chokehold fabric
of loss

HOPELESS SHAPELESS THUNDER

curse the day
you went astray
leaving me chained
fallen victim
to predators ordained

scream, i do to Zeus
throw down upon you
a lightening bolt
pierce you
make you convulse
from the jolt

you have stabbed me
i am full
like the matador
you make suffer the bull
weak, but not dead
disappointment i am fed

storm warnings
i tried to ignore
running, charging the gore
the red
wondering if it's me
who bled

curse the day
you went astray
leaving me scorned, with
hopeless shapeless thunder
signaling
heartbreak has been born

IT'S HUMAN NATURE

sleepy little metaphors
chocolate brown enticements
whirl around you

wake up, sense
my sensuality, pollinating
pistol and stamen

petal soft, moist
warm climate, perfect 10
for the spreading of your seed

follow me, onto the grass
into the flower bed
the woods
against a tree

sleepy little narcissus
spring fever gazes
upon you

wake up, grow
to great heights, penetrate
the sky, and
me

FRESH WATER MIRAGE

Lake Michigan teases
with its brandishing movement
Grand Haven sands
a pasture suitable for my grazing
i smile
as i honour the sights
surrounding my spiral perimeter
football
volleyball
Frisbee
Boule
men
boys
liquid shirts
evoke that hedonistic urge
to be windswept
into ones arms, and they
into my being
mellow fingertips
tracing flesh
like a blind man reads brail
lips, tongue
exploring with curiosity
as only new lovers do
my body
worn as a crown
lightening, thunder
shooting stars, and
the deluge
both liberates and subdues
fulfillment of the moment
impossibility of a future

THE SENSES

speak to my soul
with the lyrical chant of a chanteuse
so that i am aware
who can make your heart sing

purr to my ears
with the romantic tongue of a poet
that my cinnamon eyes make you hungry
for the sweet taste of heaven

listen with intent
to understand my rainbow of emotions
hear and heal
my cries for love

demonstrate to me
with your eyes, lips and touch
that i am the source of fuel
which ignites your passion

feel the flesh of my existence
with the hands of a sculptor
pour yourself into my unique mould
surround me with your scent

allow our combined senses to generate
a masterpiece called LOVE

BIRD OF PARADISE

place your tongue upon my scars
where twice
i've been kissed by death

remedy the alienation
from humans
isolation
i have felt

tell me a story
live my fairy tale
swim in the river of my tears

pull me out
of the quicksand
taste my fears
unwaste my years

massage this warrior woman's body
survivor of grueling battles
and love

cure my uncertain future
make a promise
please
free this dove

CURE FOR (SELF) HATRED

at the cusp of inadequacy
lies the fallacy
buried beneath the bones
of internal scrutinizing thoughts

a seemingly safe distaste
proves an uncanny waste
as the therapist attempts to loosen
the tightrope knot on which esteem walks

what's born to flourish
is disregarded and undernourished
wrapped in a non-secure blanket
abandoned at the back door of responsibility

freedom liberates the blame
allows nakedness without shame
creates courage for perseverance, and
snapshots the moments of worthwhile quality

dignity is the transgression
eradicating immune strangling repression
setting compassion on a true north course
where inner peace will thrive unabashed

respectful of solitary silence
climb the ego-constructed fence
the other side protects with magic
inviting victory of spirit at last

STIGMATA

suffering with sympathy
empathy oozing from my pores
tears of blood
crowning stigmata
i bare the sores

i cry the tears
carry the cross
bleed the sorrow
mourn the loss

cancer diagnosis
deterioration
death announcement
i'm the wandering ghost
heaven's renouncement

her scars
his fears
burdening my chest
crippling my years

heart attacked
body bruised, but
i'm the chosen steeple
weakened, yet strong
for the people

suffering with sympathy
empathy oozing from my pores
tears of blood
crowning stigmata
i will bare their sores

SOMETIMES

my words get entangled in metaphors
i ponder the prevailing tone
of the female canary, and
i wonder if my calling
is comprehended by your male ears

my heart rests in the nest built, yet
unfulfilled, longing for the breath
of devotion to flutter and surround me
curled on my cotton cloud, i believe
in the sweet promise of love

my wingspan extends
beyond the cage of my existence
i escape the doubt of others
to arrive at wishes come true
waiting there on my mate for life

your song communicates the interest
to become my bird in paradise
guard of fidelity, protector of trust
perched, ready to act
if a threat interrupts our aspiration

our liberated spirits soar
to heights we are afraid of, yet
anxious to reach
leaving behind the comfort
of a simple paper foundation

sometimes
my words get entangled in metaphors
i ponder the bewildering route
of this human female, and
i wonder if my passion
is comprehended by your male soul

LOVE IS A FABLE

it's midnight...

there is no glass slipper
never was
no charming individual fits
in my house of cinders

wickedness exists
pumpkins smashed
i'm scrubbing floors
who's got my back?

fairy tale romances
imaginary friends
flannel gowns thicken the skin
perpetuating colder hands

hair comes down
tension climbs
love only visits
in nursery rhymes

cats, not horses
carrying mice, not men
who will ride in?
take me to THE END

CIRQUE DE COLETTE

you see me
smiling
laughing
dancing about

when I catch your glance
you see
my eyes are smiling too

you want to know me
possibly love me

and then it happens...

the story of my life is played
for you
assaulting from every angle
screaming out like an opera

you don't want to be a part
of this sometimes brutal show

you exit

and the smiles in my act
must go on

THE GRIEF MEDICINE:

- RECIPE FOR GRIEF
- SPIRITUAL TRUTHS OF A DYING WORLD
- THE HOURS
- THE WHITE CHAIR
- DEATH
- BEVERLY'S SOUL
- ONE PLUS NEVER EQUALS MY FUTURE
- OOPS! I DESTROYED MANKIND
- YORKE, DEAN, VICIOUS
- GOD
- JABBERWOCKY: THE TEENAGE YEARS
- MY LITTLE DOOM
- EVERY DAY IS THE END OF THE WORLD
- AFTER EVERYTHING IS GONE
- EMOTIONLESS

By Daniel W. Gonzales

RECIPE FOR GRIEF

The pain is apropos
Of the truth, it's a good
Starting point to grief
First you mix it in the
Lovely despair with
A white wine vinegar sauce
And add a tomato
Of rage, you must let
This simmer until
The madness settles in
And the suicidal thoughts
Come to a low boil
And once these have mixed
You may find yourself
Wondering what comes next
(That stabbing pain in your heart
That's only cholesterol)
Then you add a dash of
Regret, a sliver of denial &
A great big chunk of confusion
To the mix until you cannot
Sleep for days but your soup
Of despair is almost ready!
Finally on the one year anniversary
Of your despair, you will lay
A single white rose on the ground
Then finally dish up a bowl of that
Delicious tear-filled soup and smash
It against the wall, the smell will
Linger for days and then maybe,
Just maybe you will begin to deal
With the pain.

SPIRITUAL TRUTHS OF A DYING WORLD

The loneliness is overwhelming
Like a violent wound that refuses to heal
And I cannot pretend it's not there
That it's scabbed up and not bleeding
Because the open mouth of it
Will not rest until it has swallowed me
Whole, we like to pretend that it doesn't
Matter, that we can shuffle people and
Memories and life up like things upon
A shelf but then we see a picture and
It makes us feel like vomiting because
The memory is so strong, it quakes you
Down to your very soul. That person
Who I loved will never touch me or
Hug me again until the day I'm dead
And if you're an atheist then you know
More of dread than do I because even
Though I have faith, even though I know
There is a heaven to wait, still I feel the
Pain so real, so raw because I am human
And attached to the flesh in all its earthly
Goodness, it's so easy to give up, to surrender
Your mind to the turbulent waves of humanity
And just let self-destruction do its easy work
For there are a millions ways to kill yourself
In this brave new world, whether it be pills,
Alcohol, razorblades or sex, we can even eat
Ourselves to death, suffer in the consequences
Of our actions and wish that we were abortions
But it won't change the uneasy fact that the
Ones we love have gone away to heaven
And someday you'll pick up your ticket

And the entry man will be death with
His silver scythe wondering what took
You so long and you will smile and
Remember that pain and suffering
Are just an aphrodisiac for the damned
But the true believers ride the train
Of light to its celestial destination
And find home and hearth among
The angels in the sweet blissful
Haven of the infinite.

THE HOURS

(Dedicated to Virginia Woolf & The novel by Michael Cunningham)

Even death isn't thrilling anymore
it doesn't have the same finality it used to
it drags on and on like some petulant child
begging for candy until his mother breaks
his arm. I am hungry for the grotesque
and the beautiful and the dead. I want
my life to be a parade of surreal creatures
all vying for a spot on Insanity Roe.

I've seen identical twins reap wonders with
their lust but the lust has even become a bit
of a bore because all it implies is the inequality
of the sexes and that story has been told so
many times that it's grown cobwebs on the womb.

Ordinary hours can be comforting
ordinary things like apples and pears and oranges
and razorblades but the most beautiful thing of
all is the unknown because it holds and haunts
and takes us by breath. Those long hours
of not knowing what will happen next
and i'm afraid i've gotten addicted to the fear
of the unknown, that thrill of death or slash
not knowing whether it will be the lady or the tiger
that I've forgotten how to live.

I see the silver jellyfish in the window
and I think, "there's my brain, how quaint it looks.
Why does it seem so damaged in my head?
Will it smile now? Will it repair itself or is it doomed
to self-destruction?" Then I tuck it back into

my skull and claim this as Judgment Day.
Christ is on the throne again
and hubby is late from work.

God most assuredly is a man.

Then there is the woman in the window
baking bread all day, she looks haggard
even a little suicidal, I wave to her but she
does not see me, now she is baking a cake
she writes Happy Birthday in bold letters.
The Y is crooked, she makes a feral face
of anguish, I see death in the kitchen
but then again, I see death in all things.

Then I see the future woman
the one who has yet to exist in this realm
she has a scarf wrapped about her throat
and she looks hungry for something she
can never have. She lives in the past,
the future and the present all at once
but belongs to one of them.

She is another victim of the hours.

We are all hungry here
and we need constant feeding.
What if the world never ends? we think
What if this big mess goes on and on
and on. Perhaps there is no peace
until you are done of breath.

So we comfort ourselves with the thoughts
of razorblades and bottles of sleeping pills
and stones in the pockets.

There is hope after all
a bleak sort of hope but something
to keep us going on
knowing that there is always an exit
and we are the masters of our
own destinities.

THE WHITE CHAIR

What a dull white chair this is,
It does not move.
It just sits there like a lazy whore
Hours I have sat and pondered this
Dead white chair
And still it does not give me the
Courtesy of moving.

Why doesn't it change color?
It would look better green or blue
Perhaps it should dance for me
Or turn spindly, curve up towards the ceiling
Days I have sat and watched you,
My dull white chair and still you refuse to move.

I am getting angry, white chair
I want to stab you
I want to wipe that dirty smile off your face
You look like my father
I love (hate) you
I want to kiss (kill) you
Oh my, did I just say that aloud?
I really don't know where that came from.

Now the chair is winking at me
It's got that anxious, desperate look
Like the last girl at the bar
Like the last boy in the world
Dreaming of the last girl.

The chair is flirting with me
Now we have made love

The chair and I are laying in bed together
Smoking cigarettes
We have just had two orgasms a piece
Not that we were counting.

What an exciting chair you have become
You have lived up to all my expectations
Good chair, good chair
But I can't help but wonder:
Did you change or did my mind?

It's been months now
And I haven't left the room
I have a confession to make, my sexy,
Dazzling smooth white chair:
I think I'm falling in love with you.

DEATH

Having everything one wants
Is the most sickening state I can imagine
A human being to be stuck in.

Desire is the will of nature
Poverty makes one always hungry for something
One that has it all contains no desire
His desires are vast and illusory.

When we desire nothing
Our soul slowly begins to die
It is these material things that consume us
The illusion of depth purchased on credit card
Items which contain no spirit.

I surrounded myself with golden calves
And I found no martyr in them
There is death in everything
And death is the most beautiful illusion
We have yet to break.

It is the blackness that haunts us
The idea of nothingness personified
I don't blame her for her fear
She sees the death crawling in you
She can see the more things you own
The less human you are.

BEVERLY'S SOUL

"I'll never find someone quite like you again…"
—VAST, "Touched"

You always said all my poems were about death
but now so is this one too
I didn't care that you were "fat"
(whatever that word really means)
I would have loved you if you were the mother in
"Gilbert Grape", size never mattered to me
like it does the world but you wanted to
appease them, you wanted to get the 'Carnie Wilson'
miracle cure, you told me you wanted to "fit into
their world" just like women who get boob jobs
and sell their souls to climb the corporate ladder
Everything was fine at first, you lost so much weight
so very fast, you were contemplating new wardrobes
then suddenly you died, all I remember is gasping,
strangers in your bedroom and then the light dim in
your eyes, I must have shattered a 1000 stars with
my sonic scream of grief, my father was twirling
around his cane like a madman threatening orderlies
How horrible that even that is funny in a grotesque
disgustingly all-too-real way.
Mom, I love you.
I miss you so much. My every breath is pain.
I remember sneaking candy with you in the closet
when the cousins were asleep, you let me have all the
best chocolates, it was our secret stash.
I remember eggs and toast, your beautiful golden locks
Who cares if they were dyed....
I took you for granted and i'm so sorry

I became one of those internet kids who sits in his room
making love to his computer all night, how fucking pathetic
All I did was pop in your room and say hello and goodbye
we read the same books, watched the same shows but
then it was off to me and my cybernetic escape
Why didn't we play more board games?
Why was I such a bastard when you asked me
to get you soup? You said all I wanted was
the money but I'd sell a thousand gold coins
to have you back...now your gone
and Dad's gone mad and I feel so alone
When will these tides of agony stop rolling ashore?
When people say they're sorry they never really mean it
it's all for show. Their eyes tell a different story that
says, "Glad it ain't me." But what happens when it is
you and its your mother lying there on the table
and you see her hyperventilating because she can't breathe
then suddenly a look crosses her face of confusion
and her heart stops, then you know what God really is.

ONE PLUS NEVER EQUALS MY FUTURE

the fear moves tenderly across my brow
caressing me, telling me its all going to be
all right but I know it's wrong, the fear
loves to tease me, play at lover
then bring in the needles
I have become addicted to her
the angelic darkness with her pinstripe
curls and nymphomaniacal ways
she wants to destroy me
I'm not so easy to break, I say but the
truth is I was already broken before I met you
or I would not allow myself to be abused this way
there are zebras in the kitchen, narcoleptic blue
sometimes maroon thoughts swirling about in my head
each second is an agony I dread, to live for fear
is not quite life at all but a whim.

I will surrender myself to him
Big Bad Man Death with his electric
fingernails which drip blue phosperesence
across my thigh, lamppost dead machine
toaster broken crack whore on rye
don't call me stunning, I'll only
send you for a whirl.

I am Forever and Yesterday's Girl.

OOPS! I DESTROYED MANKIND

I was born during the end of the world
my face was plastered on every TV screen
when they dropped the bomb
I still had time to say my first word, "Fuck."

Someone was dunking my head underwater
baptizing evil little me so I would go to heaven
before I died, I was fresh out of the womb
but already I was a sinner so I cried.

You see, birth is most painful on those being
born because we are released back into the world
and we forget the joy of the spirit, we are weighed
down by all this flesh.

There were sheets everywhere and good linen
wrapped around people's heads, I didn't understand
what they were so ashamed of.

I had perfect mental clarity even though I was two
seconds old and I saw all my diseases, I saw how I
would have naturally died. I saw what I would have looked
like at 24, 36, 52 and 79. I saw my wife, my children,
her womb, screams, blood and magazine covers.

My mother was cradling me in her arms
her bright pink nipples suckling me.
I sucked with the fury of a prophet.
My father was in pieces all over the floor
Yet somehow I felt nothing.

There was ringing, a song like shrieking cradles
of death, there was pride, there was ego
there were wars to be won.

As the missile fell, I felt the hunger die in me
Here I was only two seconds old, beholding the irony
of man and as quick as I had come I was gone.
Nine months saturated in the juices of the womb.
All it took was one man-made thing to catapult me
back into heaven. Perhaps I'm better there.
I never liked this world anyway.

YORKE, DEAN, VICIOUS

(Dedicated to Jonny Electric,
A rock star as yet to be discovered)

you are an enchanting little man
with strange eye-like nipples winking
at me always, your strange, syringe-like
movements bleeding into me from
the seashell of your appeal for silence
there are no boundaries here
no echoes to disturb us.
This is the listless space
where nothing really lives
and nothing really dies
I find you here, despite my hauntings
into the so-called "real world"; it's a cybernetic
delusion wrapped in tin foil. With your Jesus arms
and caterpillar brows unfolding, I feel the essence
of a captured moment breaking through the walls
of cyberspace, something is almost real now
but it's just another delusion I created in my
raw ephemeral mind. I miss the cocoon,
always sticky, spasming, lost for a ponder
before I emerge from my crystallis
and fly off into heaven.
This new utopia you have created
for me, it doesn't matter if it is real
or not because what is reality but
the essence of moments converging
into a shallow embrace, these are
only fragments of the truth, somewhere
along the way you will find me;

I will look like nothing but hide underneath
the dirt, you will have to dig me up
I will look like a relic but I have yet to exist
in some distant, malformed future
that may never be except
for the crutch of confusion
that lives in your eyes
tells me it is so.
accept your destiny
become the reflection
in the mirror, do not deny
your power, feed on them
and don't ever forget
that its all a game
life and death,
truth and madness
because in the end
the soul leaks out through the brain
and the worms waltz with the flesh
so it's all just party favors until then
anyway.

GOD

So this is what death looks like—
Carnival grin, oblique manipulation
Of the edges like some sideshow freak
With a hard-on for pain.

So this is what the world likes—
Suffering mixed with a polite amount
Of nudity defining oppression of the sexes
And that eternal riddle of the mouth
That follows its own evolution.

So this is love—
Spread-eagled, lying on the bathroom floor
Looking like Fat Elvis, all spangles
And peanut butter banana sandwiches
Spilling over spandex like deadly reminders
Of gluttony.

So this is madness—
Creative, innovation, free of abolition
Not bound by the restraints of contemporary
Society with all it's prats and pitfalls.

This is the end—
This is how the world remakes itself
In its own image and defiles its creator
But then again, isn't that what he expected us to do
In the first place?

JABBERWOCKY: THE TEENAGE YEARS

With sincerest apologies to Lewis Carroll & The Smoking Caterpillar

Although the flesh-bags love to play slither-slunk
In the doormat of the mind, I still prefer the Jabberwock
Wuck, for the rhythm is quite divine
I hear the angels are sweaty this time of year
And hell is quite cold but where the Jabberwock goes
No one truly ever knows.

We could play at riddle and anagrams all day
But if we slither-slink the Jabberwock might get past us
Another day and if the sane tither-de-thither slips
Along the jet-spine perhaps the Jabberwock will take
Pity and sing us a demented lullaby.

I saw a whore with teeth in her eyes
She was wearing a dress full of blood and excretement
But when I arrested her on the boulevard, she exclaimed
It was the Jabberwock that made her thunk this
And behave this very way.

Oh, slimy bat that I see on the ceiling
Will you drown me to no avail?
Is there no angel in the slimy-trove of gire & gimble
In the wabes of sane insanity poltergeisting as limbo?
Will no draingel swallow me soul for I
To the Jabberwock lair doth I flay?

And if the walls begin to crumble and the ceiling
Stands on its head, do the Jabberwock sleeping dream
Himself dead? And if the narcissist opens his dradel up
To the sovereign saints of future despair…will the Jabberwock
Take us up on our offer to circumcise the fates?

She eats gobstoppers like there is no tomorrow
And the burning children in the fire barrow
Go screaming in their slay games
We dream of no tomorrow
And the Jabberwock smiles.

The vorpal blade was sold on the internet
For two thousand, ninety-nine, it belongs to some
Tibetan who lives in the jungle who doesn't know
what to do with it but liked the idea of it.
If only we could track down that meditationist
And force him to play our mongoose games, could we possibly
Slay the Jabberwock dead? And if so, would we really want to?
Perhaps there is no grave for a being without physical presence or
maybe
We have no dream to dream the thing dead in hyper sleep.

There's always Las Vegas.

MY LITTLE DOOM

(For Miss Plath, on the eve of her destruction)

She got struck with an arrow through the heart
and it beat like doomsday revived
Has it really been that long since you've died?
My god, seems only like yesterday that I found
your corpse in an old paperback.

Now something gross has crawled down my throat
and it sucks like a vampire, hiding in the blood:
I think you would understand.

Did Teddy ever really love you? I mean,
really love you as you ought to have been loved?
I don't know. Maybe he was just a man.
He should have been more. He should have been
a God. Only a God could have filled your void.

Looking in your window I realize
This is what a tea party in hell would look like.

I've found something in the oven
It burns crimson and gold
It looks like Thanksgiving turkey gone terribly wrong
The children are in the den pontificating Elvis
I don't know if they can smell your despair quite yet.

Christmas time comes early, they find your corpse
underneath the tree…my god, Sylvia, you went at the right time
Did you know how terrible it would get? Chemical warfare &
blood diseases. Perhaps you sensed with your melancholy

glory the doom that would ring throughout the remaining centuries. Perhaps you fed off that future despair and turned it into a symphony.

Perhaps there are no answers. Perhaps black despair rules over us all. Or perhaps you were wrong.

EVERY DAY IS THE END OF THE WORLD

sadder than a soldier
blacker than the night
all our dreams were drown'd in a yellow-blue sky
it's too soon to heal
it's too late to help
the only thing left for us to do now
(or at least they tell us) is fight.

AFTER EVERYTHING IS GONE

It's about healing & burning
again for them
It's about repetition & lies
It's about never being able to escape our
true nature; which is to destroy
Yes, there is a heaven
Yes, there are angels
But I don't know if we can be comforted by those thoughts now.
We found our faith in shoeboxes & expensive store brands
Now we have been forced to wake up to the reality at hand
No more pop stars, no more ersatz stances on love
No more bullshit, Hollywood.
Don't you think it's time for Americans to grow up?

EMOTIONLESS

Like a typhoon, it sunk me
I was on the edge of my seat
my mouth bitter and bloody
full of deceit. I didn't know
whether to weep or to scream
I didn't know whether to laugh
or to die. My brain was empty
and full of paralyzing thoughts.
I could feel the fire on my tongue.
Something was breaking, soul wide open,
I felt bitter and angry but strangely compassionate:
Maybe the world will finally hear my voice.

- THE FALL OF WORLD TRADE
- LIVING TRIBUTE
- IMAGINE THAT
- TRUE TO FORM
- ODE TO ALEXA MADISON: DAUGHTER OF THE SKY
- MOTHER'S GARDEN
- TICK TOCK
- UNTITLED
- UNLIKELY COMFORT
- "IMPERFECT" BEAUTY
- THE FRUIT OF KNOWLEDGE
- MORTAL GRIEF
- AFTER THE FALL
- PROPAGATING I LIE
- ODD JASON OUT

By Danielle Ackley-McPhail

THE FALL OF WORLD TRADE

Fiery death
Rains from the sky
As captive souls descend
Colliding with the pillars
Of the World,
The pyre from which
The Phoenix must ascend
and Freedom withstand
Jealousy's vicious assault.
Though innocence is sacrificed
On the altar of global politics,
Democracy will not follow
In its footsteps.

LIVING TRIBUTE

Deep into the pit
the procession wends its way
in solemn silence
and remembrance of valor...
of sacrifice...
of despair.

From the depths the soulful sound
of pipers pays tribute to the fallen,
as families of the victims
denounce the ghost of terror
in the footprint of the pillars...
the pyre...
the crypt

Flags and faces
raised defiantly
to the terrorists of the world.
Our country stands,
a living monument to the memories
of our fallen.

IMAGINE THAT

Dream for a moment
Picture her languid beauty
Worship frantically
A soaring goddess
Then wake with her magic
Glimmering in your eye
Revealing to you
Like faery water
The wonders of the world
Hidden from mortal sight

Fae-touched minstrel
Play us your songs
Of immortal splendor
Color our perception
With Titania's mystique
Freeing us
If but a moment
From the mundane shades
Of life's demands
And wrap us in
In brilliant rainbow hues
With the power
To grant us our dreams

TRUE TO FORM

last night i dreamed of fuchsia clouds
i wish my soul could hear the song
of the wild leafy sea dragons
soaring among the aerial waves

i wish my soul could hear the song
made savory with the salt of evaporated tears
soaring among the aerial waves
the heart of humanity in vibrant, bleeding colors

made savory with the salt of evaporated tears
my memories of love color my perception
the heart of humanity in vibrant bleeding colors
reflects the haunting image of your retreating back

my memories of love color my perception

ODE TO ALEXA MADISON: DAUGHTER OF THE SKY

Entering this world,
Not asked for, but in no way denied
You rest beneath her breast
Lullabyed by the beat of a loving heart
You join her gently
And rest a moment and a lifetime
Truly in the cradle of humanity
Time to leave the safety
Of your mother's womb
Wrap her arms around you
In a soft farewell
Two miracles of love are wrought
With the dual birth of child and day
As you draw an independent breath
You take up your gift of life

Though as you grow
Another's arms will hold you
For this brief moment
You are just your mother's daughter
With no other to lay claim

When all else does lay in doubt
Know your mother loves you

MOTHER'S GARDEN

Every time I see
a daffodil
I think of you, mother,
and how I used to sell
your garden
to my playmates
on the way to school.

Every time I see
bearded iris
I think of you, mother,
and the trunkloads of stalks
you planted
with utmost care
as future treasures.

Every time I see
sweet petunias
I think of you, mother,
and how I used to pluck
withered blossoms
from your garden
for handfuls of change.

Every time I see
marigolds
I think of you, mother,
and how I would harvest
dried flowers
to be our seeds
for next year's garden.

Every time I see
a garden
I think of you, mother,
and how you nurtured us
as closely
filling with pride
as both "gardens" bloomed.

TICK TOCK

burning—
yearning—
desperate longing—
empty hands
and breaking heart

Come my child,
Mommy's waiting,
come my child,
now's the time.

dreaming—
screaming—
earnest pleading—
silent house,
a ticking bomb.

Come my child,
Mommy needs you,
come my child,
must be time.

waiting—
hating—
patience ending—
barren womb
and passing time.

Come my child,
Mommy's waiting,
Mommy needs you,
out of time.

UNTITLED

Sharp words
Like the edge
on a razor blade,
Cut so fine
The wound is not
Realize
Before the blood
Wells up.

Indifference
Like the surprising bite
of a paper cut
Burns and stings
with every
Act
of motion
or subtle contact.

But it is
The casual betrayal
That rips
The heart
From human breast,
Lays it
on the ground
And proceeds to dance.

UNLIKELY COMFORT

God gave me a hug today
tears streamed down my face
in ugly flaming trails
silent now that my sobs
were long spent
God gave me a hug today
did I mention
right after I killed my cat
my heart breaking
as his rumbling purr
faded away
and his bright, loving eyes
went forever dim
for the first time in months
resting peaceful
God gave me a hug today
and a few comforting words
I no longer remember
lost in guilt...lost in grief
in my heart He said well done
as He gathered Rex
off the vet's cold, metal table
into His sheltering arms
and took his pain away
God gave me a hug today
He wore gang colors
and a stranger's Latino face
as he drove off
in his jazzed up ride
but He made sure I knew Him
and in my heart He said
well done

"IMPERFECT" BEAUTY

No pale, pastel princess —
I am a dark and lively earth-mother
cloaked in deep, rich hues,
my life displayed upon my face.

No perfect coiffure of crowning ringlets —
My tresses are wild and loose
free to catch the wind and sun,
tangled by the essence of my living.

No veiled social gaze —
Look into my eyes and reflect
that the common man
is anything but common.

No pure gold heart —
Mine is of mere flesh
capable of love and hate,
in equal measure.

No graceful arms with dainty, folded hands —
Mine are open wide,
willing to embrace the world
and reach for dreams.

No waif-like frame —
I have the width of hip
to populate a nation,
and the wisdom to wait.

No proper, mincing steps —
My strides are wide
    devouring the distance
    between me and my goal.

Not alone —
I am a world of people.
    We are what is real
    in a world of false images.

THE FRUIT OF KNOWLEDGE

Ripples
in a crystal pond
dazzle a quick maiden's eye
with faceted dreams;
Haunting glimpses
of another life
another time
another world.

Bewitched
she reaches out
to cup an image
in her mortal hand,
needing more.

Caught quick,
another vision—her own—
now resides
within the crystalline
treasure trove,
coloring her world
with refracted light.

Abandoning
the peaceful grip
of routine thought,
literary Eve
clasps the hand
of inspiration's
tormenting muse;
Fickle as an English springtime.

There can be
no innocence
when one spends
a lifetime
reading the souls
of men.

MORTAL GRIEF

grey skies extend
from mountain to the winter sea,
a guide to where it ends
in the only place much colder than
my heart.

one half of the greatest whole,
casually misplaced
like a child's once-favorite toy
whose seams, one time bound by love,
now absently are picked away.

in the innocence
of subconscious self-importance
you turned from me,
with my soul still unwittingly attached,
my spirit drains away.

i cannot hate you
in your ignorance,
chilling, bitter love is all that's left-
i hate myself
that i must love you still.

yearning for the numbness
of the icy tide,
willing the darting current
to bear the memories away,
the sirens beckon me to dance.

though i cannot bring myself
to heed their call
two have died this night-
the person i once was,
and the one i pictured you to be.

AFTER THE FALL

Twenty minutes
Into a ten minute walk.

-Thump - step - throb -
-Thump - step - throb -

- Pause -

God spoke to me today.
He said: "You gonna' make it?"

- Pause -

I said:
" . . . I have to . . ."

-Thump - step - throb -

-Thump - step - throb -

He said: "How far ya' got to go?"

- Pause -

" . . . The end of the road . . ."

-Thump - step - throb -
-Thump - step - throb -

God said - smiling - :

"Take your time

. . . You'll make it."

Then God went ahead,
In a white tee-shirt
And blue jeans,

On his way to church.

And I went on with my crutches -
Halfway there.

- Thump . . .
- Step . . .
- Throb . . .
- Thump . . .
- Step . . .
. . .

PROPAGATING I LIE

Deep within I hid a truth
a fear that silvers my hair
and haunts my eyes
lurking behind my shoulder
'til I'm shrewish in my manner
lashing out at those
I hold closest to my heart
logic and desire locked
in constant struggle.

Time—not time
a crippling need
to sow the seeds of love
and harvest progeny
how cliché—a ticking clock
… a ticking bomb
a horror that each passing moment
each squandered opportunity
will find the next one barren
stealing away my ability
while amplifying my need.

Instinct can drive one quite mad
leaving teardrops on a pillow
moist with pleasure's sweat.

ODD JASON OUT

pan flutes titillate the ear
leading his thoughts
a merry chase
through decadence

an artful glimpse
of curve at breast and thigh
through tousled tresses
as shapely legs
dance to the piper
in wooden glade

fluttering hands
graceful as a butterfly
beckon a siren's call
as ancient eyes burn
with unfettered passion

unuttered
yet clearly written
in arched brow
and hints of a smile
tugging tempting lips
there is no sin
in natural order
but society is
an unnatural child

- SPEAK NO INNER DIALOGUE
- THUNDER IS SILENT
- PLIGHT OF THE BLUEBIRDS
- CARDINAL'S ROMANCE
- HUMMINGBIRD PRAISES
- THE ROYAL CARDINAL
- HAVEN'S SUMMIT
- JUMP-ROPE'S SCHOOL DAY
- EVERLASTING
- CROSS ONE'S HEART
- UNVARNISHED VIRTUES
- GRANDMA'S LITTLE BIT OF ETERNITY
- SIMPLICITY OF INNOCENCE
- DANDELION'S DIGNITY
- A DAD MEANS SO MANY THINGS

By Darla Elaine Fitzgerald

SPEAK NO INNER DIALOGUE

Create a sanctuary
in your mind. Reserve a room
only for silence. Close
the mental doors
to all prevailing thoughts.
Keep out the world of confusion.
Paint the walls
with colors of peace and harmony.
Open the windows
of your soul.

Linger there -
Dwell in the alone time.

Receive enlightened guidance.
Discover the
spiritual realm of higher energy
and well-being.
Encounter the Divine
connection to your personal universe.

THUNDER IS SILENT

Raindrops are falling.
Pine tree drinking while savoring
the water's essence.
Cascading needled branches.
View from the room of solitude and
seclusion. Window is clouded
and misty.
Mind of silence seeking
oceans of visions -
Blue deep with inner reflections.
Translucent dreams are
sailing. Floating to the islands,
hidden in the sky.
Life breath -
Inhale thoughts of peace.
Whisper serenity.

PLIGHT OF THE BLUEBIRDS

Timid, year round
tenants. Symbol of
hope and happiness. Native
cavity-nesting birds. Seeker,
hollows in decaying
wooden fence posts or dead trees.
Weathered by time and ages.

Not too distant past, residential
Bluebirds doomed
for extinction. Modernization
of society, lost treasured building
sites for their homes.

Endowment of
man-made apartments and
Bluebird trails.
Promising.
Future of species.

CARDINAL'S ROMANCE

Powerful and swift, flight
of the suitor. Celebrated by gliding
and dancing of his tail.

Ascends an Oak Tree in the
garden. Courting a lady, Juliet.
Romeo, aware of his charm.

Rejoicing,
throat embellished, flaunts
his tail like a peacock.
Wings are humbled. Swaying
to the right and swaying
to the left.

Serenading his sweetheart, long
before sunrise, until
the shadows of grayness cease
to be. Enchantment of
his songs in full exultation.

HUMMINGBIRD PRAISES

I am nature's
individualist. Leading a solitary
life of self-sufficiency.

Hiding among promising
summer blossoms. Suspended
in the air, partaking of
nectar's fuel.

Whizzing - Flitting - Darting.
Riding in my
guardian angel's pocket.

Journey of my flight, undaunted
by the wind.
Rejoicing
in my own inner guide
and timetable.

THE ROYAL CARDINAL

Wearing a scarlet crown.
Richness of brilliant plumage.
Cloak shaded with deep dusky-red.
Majestic admiration.

Elegance in motion and
freedom to soar.

Sweet songster rehearsing
ballads loud and clear.
Ear saluted with marked and
steadfast cadence.

Melodic notes echo
the promises of peace.

HAVEN'S SUMMIT

Silence
of the forest -
Sanctuary
of the intuitive mind.
Branches of trees,
arms reaching the sky.
Connection
to a personal universe.
Streams of reflected visions -
Mirror to a higher self.
Forms of light -
Radiant energy guides,
directing one's journey
toward a path of wisdom and
to purpose of life.
Listen
to the wind's whisper
of each breath taken.
Mountains between thoughts,
the unearthing of
peace and
serenity.

JUMP-ROPE'S SCHOOL DAY

Curled at my desk - last in the row
Reciting two plus two equals four
Reviewing C - A - T spells cat
Heart aching to hear my name called
Is it recess time yet?

Playground, a resort for fun
I am pulled from both ends
Wrapping myself around friends
Skipping, clapping, twirling
Flying high over heads
Quickly sneaking under feet

Whistle blowing - signal to STOP!
Stampede of innocence - first in line
Deserted, I am left all alone
Silently sitting on the ground
Is it recess time yet?

EVERLASTING

She is a heavenly gift from God
I was blessed the day I was born
Her love eternal, never changing
No stronger bond on this earth
Thank you Mom for loving me

She has a smile of sunshine
Eyes sparkle with love
Gentle as the morning dew
Falling on a flower garden
Heart made of purest gold

Gives me hopes and passions
So much a part of me
Wise and good, she molded my life
Gift of what I am
Treasured memories within my heart

She is a gift from God
Her life will never end
A mother's love is forever
She lives in everything I do
Thank you Mom for loving me

CROSS ONE'S HEART

Divine blessing, she gives the gift of life
Unconditional love from the very beginning
Teaches what love is all about
Love that understands no boundaries, no end

Warmth and inspiration, she touches the heart
Trust in truths, find beauty in life
Believe in yourself, be kind and caring
Lesson of life that giving is receiving

Pillar of strength with a heart of pure gold
Source of wisdom, creator of dreams
Sunshine to brighten cloudy days
Gentle as falling raindrops on a Rose petal

Cherished memories of life with rainbows
Her laughter, her smile and quiet times shared
My Mother forever beside me
I am her legacy, she gives the gift of life

UNVARNISHED VIRTUES

Communion of parallel perceptions
Respected fortitude of singularity

Dissension by moral implications
Alienating conduct of character
Exploiting life's skilled game of chess
Manipulation for one's royal sovereignty
Integrity wearing a majestic crown
Imposing tarnished gems of deception
Captivating shadowed visions in the mind
Illusions of honesty and forthrightness

Perpetual clock of time in passage
Fleeting mortality of being and presence
Reaching far beyond limited understanding
Searching for courage, enabling transformation

Validation of the absolute truths
Empowering the purpose of existence

GRANDMA'S LITTLE BIT OF ETERNITY

Four precious girls and one cute baby boy
Gifts of heritage, connection to the ones before
Counting my blessings in the circle of life

Innocent eyes and smiles so sweet
Dismissing my troubles and concerns
Stealing my heart with each tender touch

Sources of pride, promises of the future
Destiny in motion, guided by fate
Hold them close and love them dearly

Treasure the moments
Fulfillment of family
Counting my blessings in the circle of life

SIMPLICITY OF INNOCENCE

A baby is
teddy bears, rattles,
giggles and grins.
Soft tiny hands and
kissable feet.
Twinkling eyes that
sparkle and shine.
Smiles that melt a heart
with just a glance.
Sweet scent of powder
and a button for a nose.
Creases at elbows and
chubby little cheeks.
Snuggles in a blanket,
wishing for their dreams
to come true. Playing
with your heartstrings,
composing a song of joy
that is felt deep inside.
Forever touching lives with
their unconditional love.

DANDELION'S DIGNITY

Rooted in a camp of native green
Private First Class upon induction
Humble rank of insignificance
Unknown in numbers of profusion
Transformation of radiant energy
Presence of light - courage - strength
Worthy of a higher valued self
Four Star General in a camp of native green

Dandelion's Dignity: No Rights
Printed Magazines
Poetic Hours - will be published October 2002
Promise - will be published Spring 2003

A DAD MEANS SO MANY THINGS

It seems like only yesterday
You chased away all of my fears
Kissed my bruises and dirty face

Bear hugs and tender embraces
Held me high to touch the sky
A dad's love plays a part in life

Overflowing with warmth like the summer sun
Caring and giving, helpful and strong
Understanding heart as big as a mountain

Sentimental soul, no ordinary man are you
Inspires dreams to soar beyond rainbows
Shines with pride with each success

Passage of time, season to season
My memories of childhood to the woman I am
You are everything a dad should be and more

By Del Senkbeil

MY CRAZY DREAM

I had a crazy dream last night,
It made me laugh out loud.
I met a handsome gentleman,
Standing alone in a crowd.

Something about him seemed familiar,
But I couldn't quite see his face.
Then he turned and smiled at me,
I could feel my shocked heart race.

It was my special dearest friend,
Who lived so far away.
He made a special trip to see me,
So we could spend a day.

What a super lovely day it was!
Got to know each other well.
Would have loved to know him better,
But my alarm clock broke the spell.

TOGETHER SIDE BY SIDE

Lets walk together side by side,
Down the long, rocky road of life.
There'll be many rocky roads to conquer,
Many hours of pain and strife.

Always stay here besides me
And give me your love each day.
Cheer me when I'm lonely,
Chase all those blues away.

I'll try so hard to please you,
As we stroll thru life together.
When the sun in the sky is shining,
Or during all our stormy weather.

We'll have many disagreements, I'm sure,
Sometimes a verbal fight,
Let's vow to end them when we retire,
With a long, loving kiss 'Goodnight.

Let's be honest with each other,
So there's nothing left to hide.
Let's enjoy our lifetime together,
As we walk side by side.

MY DREAMLAND

A big full moon is shining
Thru my window tonight,
As I lay here trying to sleep,
You face is always in sight.

It seems like you're watching over me,
An angel from heaven above,
Trying to reassure me
Of your kind and patient love.

I wish you were here besides me,
Real snug in my loving arms.
So I could prove how much I love you,
And you could show me all your charms.

When I finally fall asleep, my dear,
One thing I'd love to do,
Is meet you in my dreamland,
So I can prove my love for you.

Dreams are like our tomorrows.
You'll never know what they'll bring.
If we're lucky to meet in my dreamland tonight,
It'll really make this sad, lonely heart sing.

LIFE OF SORROWS

You'll never know the sorrows,
Loving you has brought to me.
My days and nights are so empty now.
My heart will never be free.

You took my life along with you,
The night you walked away.
I begged you for just one more chance,
But you refused to stay.

I cry myself to sleep at night,
And pray for your return.
I miss your warm willing body,
For your tender love I yearn.

How can I love another?
My heart wants only you.
The way I feel right now, my dear
My life of lovin' is through.,

I don't ever want to be hurt again,
I don't want any new tomorrows.
I just want to be happy by myself,
Be free from a life full of sorrows.

LOVE SO RARE

Sweetheart, the love I share with you
Is so rare, it seems unreal.
I just could never ever explain,
Exactly the way I feel.

This love is so very different,
I'm never sad or blue.
I feel so happy every day,
Whenever I think of you.

There's something my heart keeps telling me,
'Be careful, keep it cool,
You know this love is not for you,
Don't be a silly fool.'

'But I'm not hurting anyone,'
I talk back to my heart.
'We'll never be together,
We'll always be apart.'

We share our thoughts and feelings,
Each and every day.
I feel you're right besides me,
But you're very far away.

It will never be any different,
But I can't say that I care.
I'll enjoy it while it's here right now,
This very rare love we share.

MY EROTIC DREAM

I had a very erotic dream last night.
It thrilled me thru and thru.
But, I have no idea who my lover was.
Maybe, it was you.

We were lounging on a blanket
On the shore of a glimmery sea.
My heart was filled with rapture,
As you made love to me.

The thrill I got when you kissed me,
Was oh, so new to me.
No one else's kisses
Every filled me with such ecstasy.

I could feel the beating of your heart,
As your body and mine became one.
The euphoria that I felt right then,
Could never be outdone.

The moon as not on call last night,
So your face I could not see.
But maybe some day I'll meet this guy,
Who made erotic love to me.

MAYBE I WILL FIND YOU

Maybe I will find you
Someday, sometime, somewhere.
If I just keep on looking
Maybe someday you'll be there.

How will I know when I find you,
That you're the one I idolize?
I'll just feel the love surrounding us,
And I'll see it in your eyes.

Your eyes are the windows of your heart,
I see them clearly in my dreams.
When they gaze at me so tenderly,
The dream is real, it seems.

We met in my dreams just recently,
We loved, we laughed, we kissed.
Maybe, if this dream ever comes true,
We'll realize all the lovin' we've missed.

Well, here I am still dreaming,
That our love is here to stay.
I just can't give up, my darling,
Maybe I will find you some day.

MY LOVE FOR YOU

Everything changes as the years go by.
Except some things like the color of the sky.
And the fleecy white clouds way up above,
And the chirping of the birds and the cooing of the doves.

And the sounds of the seasons, first being Spring.
And the joy and the rapture Spring can bring.
And the hot days of Summer most everyone enjoys.
And the joyful laughter of girls and boys.

And the crisp, clean air winter can enfold.
And no one really minds when the weather's cold.
Yes, everything changes thru the years, tis true.
Except these things and my special love for you.

AN ACHING HEART

What can you do for an aching heart?
I really wish I knew.
Neither a doctor or a dentist
Can offer comfort for you.

The pain it inflicts is a steady pain.
It just doesn't go away,
You feel it in the morning when you awake,
And it stays with you all day.

You talk to your heart and tell it,
"Stop! this is no good at all,"
But it's like a turbulent river,
Going over a fall.

There is no way to stop the hurting,
Except maybe, with a prayer or two.
God may be able to stop the pain
And help you see this thru.

OUR DAILY VISITOR

There's the cutest little bushy squirrel,
Who lives near our house, somewhere.
He visits our patio every day
For the goodies we leave for him there

We've had this visitor for many years,
But lately he's being quite brassy.
If he doesn't like what we have for him
He even gets quite sassy.

His food is served in a red plastic dish,
Right near our patio door.
If he likes the food we have for him,
Not a crumb is left on the floor.

When we see the dish tipped over,
We know what he's trying to say.
'How can you be so stingy?
You didn't feed me enough today.'

But when we can't even see the dish,
Until we step outside to check.
We usually find it in a corner,
On the other side of the deck.

We think we know what he's trying to tell us,
Since this happens when we've been away.
'Hey, you guys. What's going on here?
You forgot to feed me today.

GREEN THUMBS

Lets put our green thumbs together
And create a beautiful garden of love.
Where we can stroll hand in hand
Beneath the peaceful blue sky up above.

Where children can play, day after day
Without a single worry or care,
Knowing there'll always be someone
With whom their love they can share.

Where no one will ever go hungry
Will have a nice warm place to sleep.
Where everyone will help one another,
Where no one will have reason to weep.

We'll plant lots of colorful flowers
And as they bloom each year,
We'll take them to the less fortunate
And give them a bit of good cheer.

So lets get our green thumbs together, dear,
And see what we can do
To make our world a better place
And keep our love shiny new.

WHEN WE DIE

What really happens when we die?
No one will EVER know.
Do we go up to that promised land
Way beyond the blue
To spend each day in wondrous joy
And meet our loved ones too?
Or do we go the other way
To a fiery place called Hell?
No one knows, we're sure of that,
For no one came back to tell

Reincarnation is the belief of many.
How convenient that would be!
If God could just recycle us
Many more lifetimes we'd see.
Our Heaven and Hell is right here now,
Depending on how we live.
If we're kind and caring for everyone
We'll get back what we give.
So what really happens when we die?
No one will EVER know.

OUR ROSE

Deep in my heart you planted a seed,
That memorable night, so long ago.
And from that tiny little seed,
A beautiful rose did grow.

Oh, what pain the thorns inflicted,
On my faithful tender heart,
During all the long and lonely nights,
You kept us far apart.

But that lovely rose did not die.
It struggled so to stay alive.
My deep and devoted love for you,
Has helped the rose survive.

Now our rose is an everblooming one,
For you came back to me.
We'll share it's beauty and its thorns,
Thru all eternity.

YOUR OTHER LOVE

The sun is slowly setting, casting shadows ov'er the land.
While you and I are sitting on the still warm sun kissed sand.
To feel you oh, so near me, your sun tanned hand on mine
Is a memory that I'll cherish until the end of time.

But, time we have so little, dear, tomorrow you must go,
To your other love that beckons you, and why I'll never know.
You spend much more time with her, than you ever do with me.
Oh, darling, I'm so jealous of that bewitching restless sea.

She cast a spell upon you, when you were just a little boy.
From now until the day you die, she'll be your fondest joy.
I love you oh, so dearly, there's no one else for me.
So I guess, my dear, I'll always have to share you with the sea.

THE DREAM WE SHARED LAST NIGHT

I still can see you smile at me,
While the firelight was gleaming.
'I love you so,' you whispered low.
I knew I must be dreaming.

A bearskin rug, a fireplace,
Two arms that held me tight.
Oh, darling, it was heavenly,
The dream we shared last night.

You whispered that you loved me,
And then you dimmed the light.
You kissed me oh, so tenderly,
In the dream we shared last night.

The way my heart was singing,
Made everything seem right,
Our love became complete, my dear,
In the dream we shared last night.

It was just a dream, my darling,
But it filled me with delight.
Forever I'll remember,
The dream we shared last night.

- INSANITY
- IMMIGRANT
- SPARE WHEEL
- BLACKY, THE STRAY DOG
- RECONSTRUCTING
- FLOWERS AND THORNS
- RED LOTUS
- TO HAPPEN
- HALF DEAD
- YOUR ABSENCE
- I SAW YOU HANGING
- BUSIEST BUT BACKWARD
- AN ITCH AND A TWITCH
- MEMORY AND FORGETFULNESS
- GITANJALI

By Dr Henry Victor

INSANITY

Yesterday
With might and main
I labored
To diligently learn the art
Of lengthening simple shoes
For the ever expanding
Tiny feet of my little daughter

Today
I am frighteningly tormented
To discover the contemporary wisdom
Of conveniently cutting feet
To fit useless foot-wearsMade by the reigning professionals

Disagreeing
With the modern overnight professors,
I am very assertively informed,
By their cowardly counselors,
Is plain insanityFit enough only for dismissal

Ethnic cleansing
In the political arena is easy answer
For those wolfish rulers
Greedily striving to firmly establish
Corruptive power and stinking business
Instead, dealing positively, the prevailing pluralism

IMMIGRANT

Uprooting myself, and packing my belonging
Into just a small manageable size
But with a lot of hope, joy, and adolescent excitement
To encounter greater civilization, more humane humans
I am, now, an in-secured immigrant

Amusing, those few harmless in the host land,
Lamenting not their ignorance of other cultures,
In whose atlas is absent, the country of my origin; they
Excuse me, for the lack of their accent, and
Note of me, silently in heart: from distant planet, an alien

Instigate I, also anger and vengeance
Not in too many, but in few with evil and malice
To whom the whole truth – my economic welfare
Ruining their interests; and I,
Uninvited guest, to the land of plenty, imports
Diversity, that which they hate; to
Ease tension, they desire my leaving –
Room into which, for them, I am an intruder

Similar are not the other in greater number
To whom charity, but not informed by very plain
Reason for the commencement of migration,
And willingness to share their excess, the unwanted, with
Needy and poor, the wretched in sojourn,
Giving them a different identity; they gladly
Ease my burden, within their boundary
Realizing that I am, in midst of them, a powerless stranger

Gone back, I would have, to my own hell!
Unless there were those who speak truth in plain words:

Economic welfare of host-land, prime reason for opening doors;
Samaritans, they are, in the true sense!
To them, therefore, I am none but an honored guest

Uprooting myself, and packing my belonging
…
I am, now, an immigrant…

SPARE WHEEL

Sparsely used second-hand spare wheel am I
Tightly screwed down below the dark deck
Shut out of sight, sitting stoically nearer to street
I stroke, or touch not that passing path
Except in very, very rare circumstances
When one of them becomes indisposed
But only for a dreadfully short moment
Then I am tightly fastened once again
In that very same stealthily secret space
In a planet where sharing is just a concept

Sparsely used second-hand spare wheel am I
Not inside an exciting sportive automobile
But in the precinct of wheeling and dealing of divine

BLACKY, THE STRAY DOG

Blacky, the Stray Dog
Blacky, that's how my little daughter
Caringly christened Bruno, the stray dog
After months we also met his owner
That loved much, the four-legged creature

Blacky, at dawn would slip out of our yard
Even when we tied him with the strongest chord
After sun set he will need, never to be told
To keep guard of our unfenced fold

Blacky, had two homes to guard
With two titles, 'pet' and 'stray', together to hold
Daytime faithful to owner, chasing, always, any burglar
Nighttime compassion to stranger, driving, every evil intruder

Blacky, we needed so much in that garden
Closer to that lake, with no homes firmly planted
Pitched blackness was all, in night, that was seen
With tales of haunting genii that weren't benevolent

RECONSTRUCTING

With these bleak and busted building blocks
From derelict dreams of my exhausted mind
That my trampled soul has dared to dream despite
The bleeding wound in my badly battered body

This discarded child from that ruined family
That earlier neglected student of deserted village
Intends not to bend bruised knees to insolent might
Even if pushed into bankrupt economy of ghost town

With that broken pot and empty can the beaten spirit
Will continue on that abandoned boat to reconstruct
The wretched wrecked life and rebuild burnt house
Watering sun scorched plant in that parched land

FLOWERS AND THORNS

Let me neither linger
To gather flowers to keep them
Nor to walk on
Anticipating for flowers
To bloom all my way
For what is important
Is to be on my way
To my eternal home
Through the path
That life has designed
Never grudging
But always appreciating
The flowers that bloom
And thorns that prick
For they are nothing
But providence, a grace
From heaven
For my incubation and fruition

RED LOTUS

Oh, the immaculate red lotus
The queen of flowers
The seat of Buddha
Tell me, this grown-up foetus
The secret of your excellent status
In spite of the trotting trend
That you grow in the muddiest pond,
In the stinking ground

Oh, the flawless red flora
The crown of vegetation
The seat of Buddha
How is that neither mud
Nor the filthy fluid
From which you derive your nourishment
Touch not your tender petals
Nor corrupt your fragrance?

TO HAPPEN

Nothing happens
Unless you make it happen
All have happened
For you to make it happen
Sit not, thinking that will happen
Or, someone will make it happen
For that will never happen
Until you make it happen
For it only happens
When you make it happen

HALF DEAD

I was on my way from the war-zone
To the peaceful territory when I fell among
Many robbers, who stripped me,
By paying a worthless small song
For my large land and huge property
They beat me with their traditions and prejudices
That made me appear a useless alien
And went off leaving me
Half dead while they multiplied
The easy profit of my hard toil
And my careful long term assets

Many priests did pass by
And took me with eagerness
To fill their pews and coffers
The Levites too followed them
Who stood by with their pious glance
To lift me to make me support their cause
Samaritans were too many
To hire me for cheap reward
Damning me in the permanent inn
Until I finished my green papers
To clean their stinking ass!

YOUR ABSENCE

I realize your brief absence
From home to visit with your friend
Makes me a frozen dead iceberg
And I shudder to imagine that one-day,
I must, with no excuse, let you go!

Your going away
Even for a brief moment
Makes that lively home
Into a funeral parlour,
An empty house
With dead, lifeless furniture,
Along with stuffed silent dog,
Dead, motionless picture,
The painted paper flag,
And the other unresponsive creature

All these, in full, come back to life
Only when you return with your commanding
Voice that gives meaning and cheer
Transforming the empty house
Into a lovely home, making
The stuffed dog to bark and wag her tail,
While the furniture wails and groans
As you hurt and throw down your weight
And the picture begins to move
When the flag leaps to life

I realize your brief absence
From home to visit with your friend
Makes me a frozen dead iceberg
And I shudder to imagine that one-day,
I must, with no excuse, let you go!

I SAW YOU HANGING

Jesus, I saw you hanging there alone
Like truth that needs neither props nor supports
Deserted by your studiously chosen apostles and
Disowned by Peter, James and his brother, the approved inner circle

Jesus, I saw you hanging on the cross
Like a slaughtered goat for public sale
Condemned by the elders who induced the masses to 'crucify'
Convicted by Annas and Caiphas the diligent chief priests!

Jesus, I saw you hanging at Golgotha, the place of sculls
Like a criminal with no legal practitioners to defend
Beaten with cruel hands, legs and whips
Belittled with filthy motions, petitions and abuses

Jesus, I saw you hanging outside the gate with your cassock missing
Like an un-ordained ordinary layman
Accused by both religious and secular powers that wish to stand apart
Avenged by Herod, the foxy culprit, and Pilate, the cautiously benevolent

Jesus, I saw the truth hanging there alone
With neither props nor supports to ease her suffering
Jesus, I saw truth hanging on the cross
Forsaken by both the elites and the masses
When truth didn't profit them

Jesus, I saw truth hanging at Golgotha,
The meeting place for sacred and secular
Abandoned by ministers of Church and State
While truth disturbed the status quo

Jesus, I saw truth hanging outside the gate
Humiliated and defeated, ready for burial
Because truth refused to compromise

BUSIEST BUT BACKWARD

Busiest
But the most backward
Place is my neighborhood,
Seen very little change,
While, I have passed
From childhood to adult life,
Being a boy,
Collecting leaves for goat
And firewood to burn,
To a university don
And a non-stipendiary priest

Life begins here at dawn
When children and men
Occasionally, also a woman or two
Visit the leftover shrub
To free themselves of the previous day's grub

This followed by the older folk
With un-fattened cows and slim goats
To graze the almost extinct grass
Then come those who catch fish
By stirring the stagnant pond
While the underfed stray dogs
Keep annoying the already frightened goats
Chained to their fixed posts

Towards the evening
But, only if there is no gun firing
The boys will be seen playing
Re-confirming, and re-confirming
The absence of my neighborhood's matriarchy

Later as the sun sets
The younger from among the older
And sometimes, even
The elder from the older
Trickle towards this busy camp
For cheaper but illicit strong drink
Patronized by the state's law enforcing machine

Busiest
But the most backward
Place is my neighborhood,
Seen very little change,
While, I have passed
From childhood to adult life

AN ITCH AND A TWITCH

My window curtains are wide open
I'm watching people on road ahead
Bound for some work, or returning home
With groceries and drinks for their kid

My mind too is not truly closed
I'm thinking thoughts of spotless gold
Bold and eternal, surviving coldness
Like that of Frost and Service of old

My spirit too is not in that rest
With many an itch and a lot of twitch
Like that damn deer dancing near the road
Finally killed by that my stupid car

MEMORY AND FORGETFULNESS

I'm amused and amazed by your solitary heart
From which, both my memory and forgetfulness
Flow into mine as your sacred gift, and a trust
That I need to employ in all my wakefulness

I'm baffled and bemused by those contrary elements
Operating within me, simultaneously, to embrace and reject
You, the prime source for my holding tight and that negate
Of your negating my negations of you and your rudiments

I'm certain and confident in your inclination for plural
Ways of dealing with that color and creed, both in multiple
That I will find special favor among yours, not unequal
Among the other, affirming that mine is never too little

GITANJALI

Gentle you were, in your smile
Involuntarily shaking limbs, until your
Tiny frame, into my hands, it slipped
Amusing me with gorgeous amusements
Negating in me those moments of meaninglessness
Joyfully, with tiny fingers
Affecting more life into my faltering being
Like the season of spring
Invigorating the shuddering mother earth

Vanished with your birth were
Ills that crippled us for fourteen years
Causing us to sing those songs
That makes God leap and dance!
Overwhelmed by a sudden birth, and
Remembering Tagore, we named you Gitanjali

- **SCREAMIN' LISA**
- **SENSE OF PRIDE**
- **TWO WORLDS**
- **UNBROKEN ARROW**
- **BATTLES OF THE HEART**
- **THE GAUNTLET**
- **BEDOUIN SIN**
- **CHILDREN OF THE SUN**
- **ECHO OF THE MOUNTAIN**
- **FREE WORLD SOLDIER**
- **GONE IS THE DAY**
- **WARRIOR'S SONG**
- **WIND AND FLAME**
- **POET'S LAMENT**
- **RESERVATION SUNDOWN**

By Herbert L. Burd

SCREAMIN' LISA

She say's her name is Lisa,
like it's something more than a name.
My name is Lisa,
the one that's left to remain.
Half is the sun, the other half is rain.

They say the good die young.
Must be a reason why we're here.
Why we are here.
Why is not exactly to very clear.
Lisa knows, Lisa knows.
Come across many doors,
some are open, some are closed.

What was the present is now the past.
What was the past is now the present.
People in this life have been such a trip.
Some you don't remember,
some that you can't forget.

Turquoise is the moon.
She rides a painted pony.
Time means nothing to Lisa.

SENSE OF PRIDE

They say that the
pen is mightier than
the sword.
Yet question the
rhyme and reason for
all of the seasons.
The question of love
between a man and a
woman,
still remains a
question.
Sometimes the river
grows wider
yet has it's own
sense of direction.
When you become one
within yourself,
knowing that there
is nowhere to run
and nowhere to hide.
Understanding truth
in one,
what remains is what
was already a given,
a strong sense of
pride.
And the wind still
lies unexplained
a mystery and a
legend in all of
folklore
that has been voiced

in all generations.
Wisdom that I seek
has already been
written
yet somehow
forgotten except in
spirit.
The moon and I dance
to a different sense
of rhythm.
One from the sun and
walks in balance
known as wisdom.
One day you may know
of these things.
How is your heart
today?
So I say again,
how is your heart
today?.

TWO WORLDS

I hear the drums
beating
The drums have words
of their own
Sometimes they are
speaking
Sometimes they are
silent
Because they are
from a world of
their own
Do they speak to
you?
Can you hear?
Can't you hear?
For you are the
spirit's always
near?

I'm caught between
two worlds
It's not good or
evil that you and I
have always been
told
I'm just caught
between two worlds
Always seeking
warmth to escape the
cold
I'm one from two
worlds

Two worlds.

The running blood in
my veins
From the sea to the
wind
All the animals that
be
I'm one from the
land of the Katlet
Clan
of the Cherokee
Cherokee.

May I speak to all
of the other tribes
To the Nation of the
Apache
To the Nation of the
Lakota Sioux
To the Nation of the
Comanche
May I speak to all
of you
As well as the
tribes of the Amazon
And all of the
shadows of the sun
May I speak this one
from two worlds
Two worlds.

Some say the arrows
are broken
But true vision is
much deeper than

that
Words are words but
the spirit's words
have
yet to be spoken,
spoken
The spirit's are a
part of you and I
Of course we always
ask why.

So why am I one from
two worlds?
Two worlds must I
live
I've learned not to
forget
But yet I've been
given the strength
to forgive.
Being one from two
worlds
Two worlds
My blood is mine
But is from two
worlds
I am happy that the
drums beat for me
One from the Katlet
Clan of the Cherokee

Speak to me all the
tribes of our Mother
Earth
Should we forget our
past?

Pay no attention for
the present?
Disregard and
neglect our future?
Should we forget the
nature of our blood?
For what then are we
really worth?
One world, two
worlds, how many
more

No more
No more
Yet the drums are
beating
Beating
Beating in two
worlds
My world
Your world
My world
Two worlds.

UNBROKEN ARROW

Should I give you my knife.
Should I become your sacrifice.
I will stand before you.
Do as you wish to do.
But then again I'm not your fool.
I stand an unbroken arrow.
Unbroken arrow.

It is true I wore their uniform.
But what else could I do,
for that is all that I've seen since
I've been born.
I dream of running through fields of corn.
John Law and I just do not mix.
I can see through all of their tricks.
I stand an unbroken arrow.
Unbroken arrow.

Some fly with the Eagles.
Some fly with the Sparrow.
But I stand alone.
Red spirit and bone.
I stand an unbroken arrow.
Unbroken arrow.

Me and my James Dean ways will
never change.
Look at you, look at me, and you
call me strange.
Your laws don't apply to me.
I am strong and unbound
always to be free.

One with eternity as destiny.
I stand an unbroken arrow.
Unbroken arrow.

I do not care for the nature of your blood,
for you have left your mark behind.
You have left your mark behind.
You think that you know me,
when you don't know me at all.
When I am one of the wind.
I've seen times again and again.
Yours is just another kingdom that
I'll have to watch fall.
I stand an unbroken arrow.
Unbroken arrow.

Some fly with the Eagles.
Some fly with the Sparrow.
But I stand alone.
Red spirit and bone.
I stand an unbroken arrow.
Unbroken arrow.

BATTLES OF THE HEART

The wind tears at my
soul.
The open road
sometimes is
the only way to go.
And the worlds
conscience you know
will never lay to
rest.
What is left behind
just becomes second
best.
Winners and losers
are all the same.
In a world of
nothin' but smoke
and flame.
When it comes to
when the tears stop
to start.
Then you will know
that your in for a
battle of the heart.

When you know that
your love
is in someone else's
arms.
There's no gun or
anything else
can do you anymore
harm.

Closed doors and
closed minds.
I pray to the
spirit's to unleash
mine.
And the wind tears
at my soul.
The open road
sometimes is the
only way to go.
When it comes to
when the tears stop
to start.
Then you will know
that your in for a
battle of the heart.
I stand on top of
this mountain trying
to see as far as I
can.
Waiting for love to
come and take me by
the hand.
Maybe one day this
world will no longer
be
just another foreign
land.

THE GAUNTLET

We're born into this world with the gauntlet to travel down
Never knowing the nature of it's design
Twilight zone remedies so profound
You have your's and I have mine
Sometimes the rain doesn't matter at all
We never know, like a boxer, when to take a fall.

We just keep on traveling taking the hits
Don't bother counting the scars that your trying to forget
We are just a high wire act without a net
I'll walk, I won't run, down this gauntlet given me
If I should fall, woman, would you save a kiss for me?
What we leave behind is just life's legacy.

But you won't know if I've come or gone
Down this gauntlet, I'll keep pushing on
We travel with no warning signs ahead
Or do we just disregard them?
We just travel on wondering when this gauntlet will end
Maybe it does not end at all
Where did it all begin?

Wind carry me on
Carry me on.

BEDOUIN SIN

I am one,
destined to travel the desert plain.
I am one,
where the sand is the rain.

Sometimes sleep during the day.
Make my journey in the night.
I let the stars lead my way.
North star lead my way.

In the heat of the day,
when the mirage's come.
I'll wait for her, my lover,
for she's the one.

In the still of the night,
I can only dream of her.
I can't wait for tomorrow to come.
I hope to see her again,
for she's the one.

I wish I could travel with her.
For she's the one.
When mirages come.

CHILDREN OF THE SUN

Ancient times of long ago
Lies the answers that we need to know
Temples raised up to touch the sky
People dressed like they were ready to fly
Answers to many things lie deep within the eye
We are the strong ones
We are the rivers that run
We are the chosen ones
We are the children of the sun

We are all related somehow
What was red is now blonde
What was clear is now black
Doors that were open are now closed
Where there were answers now lie question

Where kings reigned now fools exist
What was truth now is lie
Bring me back to true love
Open again the heavens above
When the journey is done
Return, children of the sun.

ECHO OF THE MOUNTAIN

Here my spirit is at
peace,
surrounded by the
many gifts from
heaven.
A sense of
tranquility, a
comfort,
that comes from
within.
I sit and listen for
the wisdom of the
wind.
Though I seek
isolation,
I am not for I have
the company of
nature.
I walk along her
path with the hawk
flying
over my head as if
to guide me.
Truth I thought lost
is not
as I walk among her
beauty.
I am one that will
forever heed to
the echo of the
mountain.
No matter where that

I might be.
I pray for the
balance of life.
For it is here that
the
masks of deception
are gone,
and I'm closer to
the touch of
immortality.

FREE WORLD SOLDIER

I believe in living on a mountain of peace
I believe in the words the wise ones teach
I believe in Mother Earth to protect me
I am also here to protect her that's how it's meant to be
I believe in the meaning of the word free.

You may not know my name or my face
You may not know my religion or my race
Even though all sister's and brother's are we
Living in one world, a belief in humanity
I dream of the day living without weapons,
yet living in a world of liberty.

A disease has come and has darkened the sun
A cure must be found once again the war has come
I too will take my stand,
to maintain the freedom of every child, woman, and man
Free world soldier our flags are hand in hand.

When all is said and done
When we see the return of the sun
Once again we will return to our lands
Free world soldier our flags are forever hand in hand
For freedom will never be out of reach
Then we can rebuild Mother Earth's mountain of peace.

GONE IS THE DAY

The river's are crying into the sea's
Silence has over come countries and cities
Shooting stars are flying through the skies
Look at the Statue of Liberty how she cries
But the flag of freedom still proudly flies.

Candles are burning all over the world tonight
A dark shadow has fallen over the twilight
There's a stillness which is heavy in it's weigh
Playground's where children used to play
Is calm now, for gone is the day.

Madness has come and shown it's face of tragedy
Touched by cowards hero's they are not to be
Gave us such a dark day in human history
People working hand in hand with no words to say
Free world stands in dismay, for gone is the day

Gone is the day but not forever
Price for freedom a high one to endeavor
Candles are burning all over the world tonight
A dark shadow has fallen over the twilight
But our lady liberty's torch will always be burning bright.

WARRIOR'S SONG

My winds are not like yours
I am that of the four
Understanding of the earth
The blood of my birth
Have we met once before?

Animals of the land and sea
Part of you is a part of me
Are you of the day or of the night?
Have you flown with the eagle in flight?
Are you here for all eternity?

Upon the pedestal of life I stand
Time passes me by
Destiny a grasp within my hand
Fate awaits with a silent sigh

Have the stars ever spoken to you?
Does the river flow through your veins?
Have you walked upon the flame?
Are you the sun? Are you rain?

Are you the present or the past?
Have you walked where the shadows are cast?

WIND AND FLAME

She satisfies my complicated soul
With love there is so much to know
Simplicity out of reach
Left stranded on this isolated beach
She stands with me.

Crossed over the border a long time ago
The inner child takes control
Does not care where this river flows
Wild revelations and she knows
In all the turbulence she stands.

Traveling like the wind
A ship way out to sea
With love and all of it's honesty
She holds the flame.

He's the wind
Where all things end and begin
She's the flame
Passion and all it's glory
He's the wind
She's the flame.

POET'S LAMENT

I'm being weighted down,
with all the things that I see.
I don't know why,
this is happening to me.
There is no meaning,
for the word free.
Why did the spirit's choose me?

I hear the rain forests crying.
Right before my eyes,
I see my world dying.
Where is life for us without
our environment?
There is no truth to any federal
government.
I'm being weighted down,
with the poet's lament.

They say that space is the final frontier.
That won't be any good,
if Mother Earth is no longer here.
I wait for the day that I can see
the oceans smile again.
For me, this lament, has no beginning,
the poet's lament has no end.

When it's time for my circle to close.
I'll return to the wind.
It will be time for a new life to begin.
But only to carry the poet's lament
once again.
Always to have a new beginning,
but there will never be an end.

RESERVATION SUNDOWN

Sittin' by the river with bottle in hand.
Underneath this bridge that was once called the promise land.
From border to border not much to do.
Broken treaties is the only truth ever spoken to you.
Underneath this bridge I guess I'll make my final stand.

They pushed us back and gave us what they could not use.
They murdered us saying their law was the excuse.
The truth was greed with land and gold in their eyes.
What they did not know a warrior's pride never dies.
Some prefer to take a stand and watch them light their cannon's fuse.

They say that the rain never comes here.
Like the water in my eyes a long forgotton fear.
So I'm here underneath this bridge questioning
the courage of death and life.
I still stand unbroken even though disease came
and took my children and my wife.
Puzzeled by question's all answers some time are not always clear.

The sun now is slowly fading down.
My bottle now empty I toss upon the ground.
Left with an empty feeling once a rich history.
Now is sold on the corner the art of my people's legacy.
Once rich in wisdom now can be hardly found.

- SOME STONES HURT
- SCAR TISSUE
- DOWN THOSE STAIRS
- SUDDENLY IT'S SOLITAIRE
- SONNETS IN A LAND OF PROSE
- LIKE BRIE
- THE LIFTED SKIRT
- THANATOPSIS
- WATER & LIGHT
- DOUBLE VISION
- CAMELS & SAND
- SEEDS BEHIND THE STORM
- SCREWS THAT HOLD
- SLOW DANCE ON THE KITCHEN TILE
- SOUTHERN HANDS

By Janet I. Buck

SOME STONES HURT

I was ten years old
when I saw the Venus de Milo
posing on clean gray tile.
Shutter clicks were going off
like car alarms.
And I was ashamed of her stone.
Of the air where her arms
were destined to be.
I wondered why she had no scars.
If she hated the eyes —
their rabid dogs, their
pigeon-dropping cloying orbs.
I wanted to give her my clothes.
Pass her a bottle of glue.

"She's broken," I said to my aunt.
"Why is she here — in a place of respect?"
No answer emerged from her tongue.
I thought about my missing leg,
its carcass and its animal.
Later I would share her shape.
Duck cameras like a waiting knife
pressed to a throat of crumbling sand.
She must have taken a fall.
"Someday we'll chat," I said to her,
"over a meal of oysters and art
about the presence
of grit in the shell,
about the impotent rage."

SCAR TISSUE

Your body crossed the busy street,
one long and wrinkled leather scar
hitting sockets of marble eyes,
refusing entrance to your grief.
Spinning with their obligations
chipped by hands that clanked on clocks,
confined by fear, deflecting fate
from striking at their sanity.
Your walk was slow,
slug trail after pounding rain.
That trudging pain I understood
from hoofing on a bleeding stump.
But I had clothes to cover up.

You pulled at rims around your hat
as if your flesh were slips that show
on necklines of an evening dress.
I pondered both our legacies.
Mine was just a missing foot,
an absent knee, a choppy limp
unraveling the upper curl of impish smile.
Still alive and waltzing a disjointed dance
to chances that tomorrow's lot
would bring less salt of agony.

Your life a jerking rattlesnake
that ticks beyond its mortal span,
constricting to the cruel beat
of something denser than a man
should ever be anointed by.
Orange suns above your head
had to be, just had to be tiny reminiscences

of flames unwelcome for their sparks.
Struggle was an Armageddon
larger than a movie screen.
Horns just blared in such impatient unison.
I wanted to scream, be the cradle of an angel,
make my loudness carry you
to safer places than this world.

DOWN THOSE STAIRS

The basement was always locked,
locked tight as a nut in a bolt.
From here the magic grew,
a guess gone wild,
a brothel of abandoned hours.
Having nothing to say,
we pressed our ears to the walls
until a story, a ghost
dropped seeds for inquisitive eyes.
Sweating like glasses dripping in heat,
we parted the cobwebs,
their living room drapes —
knew by instinct tied to time,
this place was a sunken ship
where chandeliers once burned
their tenuous suns.
A million crevices and caves,
eros of a question's lid,
underwear drawer of a house,
forbidden but calling our hands.

Bridges we found to the sea —
piers of an ancient storm.
A dusty chair missing a leg,
someone's palsied, pilfered dream,
its cushion a tongue
that spoke with silence and tilt.
Too young to embrace satin dark,
accept an unanswering world
of strapless luggage,
boxes wet from a flood
like faces in an old folk's home,

a dirty handkerchief that knows —
we listened for marching mice,
making the best of jetting
across their little roads.
Here the beams were odysseys —
rod and staff reduced to twig.
We left the door of fear ajar
so tiny streaks of light could talk.
On the other side of the slab
colors were even and clean —
drafts of red spaghetti sauce
promised us no poverty.

SUDDENLY IT'S SOLITAIRE

One moment he's pruning a wayward branch;
garden tools rest happily against
the brick like spoons in soup.
You wonder how it stayed this warm.
An ancient sun is baking leaves, raisins
in a rising dough of seasons on a schedule.
He edges grass the way he's always
sculpted love — by doing things
in steady gestures like the rain.
A seizure, then a surgery.
Then solitaire so suddenly.
Feet aren't there to track rich soil;
welcome mats have lost all words.

I bake two pies and take
two pieces down the street.
It's a short walk and a long hill
up to the crown of thorns.
The first thick snow is blowing
blizzards of his death as if
some crazy heaven dropped a sack of flour
and all the meals I'm handing you
are just reminders of the cold.
I ring the bell, its tired fly
catches in the vivid freeze.

A single place mat at the bar
stares back at us as if
no cards but this exist.
Boots are empty lecture notes
reminding me that luck
is amputated by the hour.

His coat is hanging like a ghost
beside a hat that buckles
in our winded sighs.
A living room of Roman girth —
spotless but for photographs
you finger in the night's abyss.

*First Published in **Black Creek Review**

SONNETS IN A LAND OF PROSE

"Between my head and my hand, there is always the face of death."
Francis Picabia (1878-1953)

Christmas lights have decked your house
for eighteen months
as if you're hanging cherry pits
of a futile wish, plastic
sprigs of neon green
to drown the immutable dark.
His truck still sits on vulva ruts —
mosaic mud — an albatross
in sprawling jungles of yellow grass.
Death and love are always
messy taffy pulls.
Everywhere your fingers reach,
some brand of thanatopsis lives.
His garden tools all vices of a memory.
If graves are just a dry tureen,
why do they adhere like tar,
turn forward into festered wounds?

You save his voice on mini-tapes.
Listen to its orchestra
for sanding down the silences.
Use it like a sleeping pill
when clocks become a ticking bomb.
His pipe still packed with fragrances
you hated then and now embrace.
His baseball hat is nesting birds
in cradles of a fallen oak.
Every time I bring the mail,
your housecoat wears the painted tear,
its canvas tired and shrinking

as the grief grows tall.
You read his name like sonnets
in a land of prose.
His *Lazy-Boy* just looks at you —
a boulder in a hollow cave.

*First Published in **Stirring Magazine**

LIKE BRIE

Meat locker death is a shivering place
made mostly of hooks,
torn, torn guts of equipoise.
I was plastic towel racks with lousy screws.
My walls of strength were all charades.
There it was: the hailstone,
bigger than the street it hit.
I should have been there
to hang and tilt paintings
of your last drawn breath.

From windows of an empty house,
a sunrise looks like sauerkraut,
sunsets mimic refried beans.
There was hidden color here
in splinters of remaining wood.
You went like brie exposed to air —
too fast for tongues
to lick the richness from the rind.
I was busy with naive,
asking for the picnic back,
coaxing tulips through hard ice.

Later I would gather
crumbs inside a poem.
Its checkered tablecloth for bags
to seal away unwanted fumes.
My visits short and squatty rites —
crew cuts on a shaggy dog
I was too lazy to bathe.
Sagging corn husks of your hands
were meant to be the braided art

that dresses up a lonely field.
Even in your suffering,
gifts you left deserved my lids
forked open in this wilderness.

*First Published in **Unlikely Stories**

THE LIFTED SKIRT

After your death, I stare at your bed —
robot in a stony igloo wanting
to trade the chill for warmth.
I smell your hair in pillow conch,
in feathers of abandonment
that take a fragile world by storm.
I look for oysters in a clam,
for pearls on a broken chain.
Mourning's ugly odyssey
keeps turning up the slaughtered dream.

Beneath the skirt sit tumbleweeds —
dented slippers, empty boxes,
spoons and forks and tea cups
with a lipstick mark that used
to sue a cloudy day with stripes
of sugared grenadine.
A messy maze of cords and wires
all attached to nothing much
but sockets of recurring grief.
A cactus counting water drops.

I finger webs for widows
which I know will bite
or drive me to a whiskey glass.
Run across the lint of lonely
decked in golden lion fleece.
A stethoscope through which
I hear my clawing heart,
fossils of a rose's womb
that never made it to a vase.

The waffled mattress bears your prints,
urine-stained with facts of time
no catheter of need could change.
A diaphragm for sex with fate
that didn't work, our prayers
had holes no funeral mass
or black cortege could staple shut.
Air stays fonts of stale gin —
some sterile note of punishment
for loving in the first degree.

*First Published in **Literary Potpourri**

THANATOPSIS

"Death destroys a man; the idea of Death saves him."
-E.M. Forster (1879-1970)

Time just broke like fishing twine.
Fear became our very breath.
A book louse eating scrolls
of prayer and sacks of flour.
Death's dirty needle struck our veins.
Drip. March. Drip. March.
Ash, thick, ash; smoke, dense smoke.
The ground sits like a friar's cape,
dormant and rough, coveting
these nervous metrics,
gnawing reefs of labial coral —
pink, inviting, cognizant
of circles coming to their ends.
I'm counting on the sun to climb,
but all my eyes are focusing
on what's inside a passing cloud.
Ground hogs say the winter
still has tricks ahead.

Spring just swerves from lane to lane.
Terror and its ventifact
rattled all our absolutes,
froze whatever arrogance.
It's up to touch to bring
this glacier to its knees.
Shadowboxing hatred's wind is testing us.
Seas seem larger than the swim.
How much muscle do I own?
Will urning the dead,

Will urning the dead,
slipping change in widowed pockets,
give this earth its wholeness back?
Will listening stop mourning bells?
Will faith in little things return?
Will questions plain exhaust their curves?
Too late to plant a tulip bulb, my mother warns.
I stand, boot on shovel's razor edge,
insisting I can split the stone.

*First Published in **The Pedestal Magazine**

WATER & LIGHT

The war is in our living room,
yet tucked behind the luxury
of polished glass.
I'm folding laundry on the couch,
watching soldiers storm a city,
spinning sand behind their wheels.
Tortures and catastrophes
are miles and continents away.
Villagers are shredding posters
with their knives — all my prayers
converge to hope they're opening
ripe liberties as melons split
and serve themselves to thirsty lips
lying in timorous wait.

How fortunate that I can
study human sorrow
through this scope, retreat
without a broken neck
to tortoise shells of urban life,
seat myself at a table
scattered with food.
I have water, hot and cold,
lazy Susans full of rice;
I have lights for reading lamps.

To test myself, I work by
tiny candle flame —
close the valves that ferry
liquid through our home.
I go without a morning shower,
quickly start to hate my smell.

I am not that little boy on CNN
with diatribes inside his eyes —
lamenting vacant space
once filled by reaching arms.
How fortunate for pale hands
to grab a narrow black remote,
mute the echoes of the guns,
wash away the silences.

*First Published in **Adagio Verse Quarterly**

DOUBLE VISION

In theatres of roiling dust,
one photo shines
above the desert's milky cast.
A PFC cradles an Iraqi boy
wounded during heavy battle
near Al Faysaliyah.
All four sleeves wear stains of blood.
This portrait is sharp
in reply to the cyclone of terror.
We promise them water and food.
Some eyes see our troops as sharks
that follow only scents of oil —
others see us bearing loaves
of bread to split among
the caves of hungry mouths.

I grab at hope and pray
we fill these wishing wells
with rivers of pure sacrifice,
all the while aware of truths
that lie in wait in caskets
and in mourning robes.
As bullets fly, as whipping berms
mix corpses laced with uniforms
and weapons protrude
like twigs on fallen trees,
I stretch to see entire wars
through lenses of this renaissance —
a ballet move of pointed toes
in quicksand riding to my chin.

*First Published in **The Pedestal Magazine**

CAMELS & SAND

A strange mélange of curves
against the thorns and barbs of war.
Dog-eared berms wrestling
with another storm.
A soldier sleeps against
the barrel of his gun,
dreams of cherry trees at home.
A white picket fence inside this world
is concertina wire and guards
in suits of glaucous camouflage,
bombs for crickets
singing in the evening light.
Camels pass in dusty colors,
their instincts blend
with parched terrain —
they're born prepared —
and we are not.
Sand is all the grass they know.
They wander by so casually,
an orange sunset at their heels.

*First Published in **Tamafyhr Mountain Poetry**

SEEDS BEHIND THE STORM

A few stray palms huddle in dust.
A street is a dirt road
needled with leftover guns.
The bridge has been bombed,
then patched with precarious rocks.
All carriages nervous
with crotchety wheels.
Maybe a goat will make it home.

Both sides of something called war
are fragile and tired.
Your breasts, two going Comice pears,
hang over your dwindling ribs.
The wind blows on
in unforgiving gusts.
Your veil still whole and black
against the thinning ropes of light.

SCREWS THAT HOLD

"Just shoot me," I say,
as I'm straining to stand
like sunflower necks
crippled by storm.
They give a horse that courtesy
in wounded times.
When the pain, its mercurial bead,
rises its ball up in the glass,
I know its tumor swells in you.
My laugh is a hair in your eye
growing crimson from the watch.
It's been five years —
broken this and tortured that
with scalpels for our silverware.

Most men in brutal hours like these
would be a lousy towel rack
leaving walls from too much weight.
You deserve to flood the room
with thick exhaust
from tailpipes where anger smokes.
I wonder why you never do,
but hardly question constancy.
We spoon at night.
Ripe apples of your giving knees
remind me the tree is there,
its roots a map I stretch to read.
These casualties of carnal war
are worth the bijoux and the crown —
sweet trouvaille of one last dance,
under sharp claws of the stars.

SLOW DANCE ON THE KITCHEN TILE

The last time we talked was in
the center of death's wadded fist.
Its nails were digging into our hands.
Pain drifted words off cliffs —
alyssum seeds in wide-mouthed
canyons living off that cruel wind.
Shrunken mangers of a moment
lit by flames and up in smoke.
Neither of us recalls the meat,
just omnipresent sense of blood —
his pale, waxen face
in the open casket our tears
tried hard to close and lower into memory.

In the context of a widowed flower,
I hesitate to share sweet news
of slippery palms on passion's
doorknob turning at the speed of light —
when yours is grains in tilted urn,
instant coffee set beside my deep,
brown, whole beans, wafting
through the heating ducts.
But you ask, so I spill. Hoping the liquid
won't leave a crust you'll have to scrub
when I start my car and you sit silent
on the couch, on cactus thorns of longing rites.

"Is he a hugger and a holder?"
you pry. My luck, my blessings
glisten on a wetted tongue.
"He is and more. Our nights and days,
together's press, are love letters

from a cat to a can of tuna fish."
All dead end streets forgotten
for oasis second in blowing sand.
For you are the prism of cherishing
and I am willing prisoner.
We'll slow dance on the kitchen tile
even in the shadow of the valley of death.

---

*First Published in **Kimera**

SOUTHERN HANDS

It's a cold place for Southern hands
bent on rain rust and the creaking chalice
of a porch swing, its sure-footed hymn
miming an assenting breeze.
Negligée arms of gray willows
whisk the scraps of her missing scent.
The sun's lemon reduced to rind.

You see again a lawn to mow,
tall shrubs to clip, her garden shears
inside her hat, old tablatures of studded dream.
She was the pen and you were the page —
chapters bound by wedding rings
that circumcised most tragedies.
Quills she was still tickle flesh,
then turn to needled porcupines.

That was there and this is here.
The desk is stacked with patient charts.
Nurses in white masquerades
pass in their cake-walk smiles, frozen in sincerity
like salesmen at church bazaars.
You clutch the walker and push, its silver teapot
metal rails no mimic of those better times.
Insisting the phone, trilling its wail, will be for you.

You ask, weakly, for a map to "Home."
'H' hisses like a pile of snakes.
A guilty voice drums her practiced protocol:
"This is home, it's wonderful."
Clichés clicking on her teeth.
"It's NOT!" you say, "I smell like piss.

We had ambrosia petals there."
She reaches out and curls a tress,
a wiry weed around your ear, pretending
she has magic tricks hiding under cuticles.

She shoos you to the elevator's grimy shield,
its weak asbestos crumbling.
Her pager beeps; you almost fall asleep to birds.
She slugs the "Up" button with her fist,
mad at sorrow's acreage, as you tap "Down"
and nod, then blink. Your Southern hands,
now withered prunes, playing the plum
like a scratched record
on a hoarse and dusty phonograph.

*First Published in **PoetryBay**

- GOING PLACES
- INSIDE THE ACTOR'S STUDIO
- A CHOICE ENCOUNTER, A MOMENT OF ENLIGHTENMENT
- 12 IN THE AFTERNOON
- IT DOESN'T GET ANY BETTER THAN THIS...
- 3 AM WAITING
- GOOD LUCK, HALF-HEART
- THE MUSICIAN
- THAT MESS ON THE SIDEWALK
- IT WAS IN A 45
- ONE FOR THE ANALYSTS, ONE FOR THE EXAMINERS, ONE FOR THE SCRUTINIZERS AND PICK-APART ARTISTS

By John Dempsey

GOING PLACES

Headed for the madhouse, the poorhouse, the sidewalk, a jail cell, an early death, some sprawling three story on the west coast, maybe overlooking the water, 2 cars in the garage, the young drunken wife and a chain gang of children, sure, it's right over the next horizon…

(Unexpected weight on my chest this morning, I felt I was missing something; I had dropped something, forgotten something- but what?
Turns out I wasn't breathing.
Life!
Life hid in my shirtfront pocket.
Bitch was disguised as a government issued check for 661 dollars and I had her by the throat. I had her by the throat with 2 inches to spare. I had her by throat and that bird wouldn't be singing for a while. I started breathing. Called in sick to work, dressed and made it out the door.)

Headed for the bank, the unemployment line, the welfare office, an early death, some awards ceremony for the Pulitzer prize, dressed sharp in a 3 piece designer suit, monogrammed handkerchief peeks out from the pocket, a gold watch, on a gold chain, dangles real aristocratic like, sparkling and gleaming, reflecting tiny bits of aristocratic light, sure, I can see it all now…

(Dressed and made it out the door. Hit the street thinking about problems; I've got tons of them- who doesn't?
Show me a man with no problems and I'll show you a man in a coffin.
Life!
Life is all about dealing with problems.
A major problem is with self-importance. We all have an image of ourselves that exceeds the concrete, an image that blasts us off the sidewalk of the ordinary…upstairs,

we're all the next big thing, the next name up in lights, the next icon to hit the stage. Shit! I cashed the check and bought an egg sandwich. Ate the thing on a bench in the sun. It was about 60 degrees out.)

Headed for skid row, the free clinic, the rehab, a detention center, an early death, some small corner in the Lit section of your local bookstore signing copies of my latest literal catastrophe, teenie bopping readers with long hair and nose rings squirm and sweat, standing on line with a scent coming off their crotches. I pat one on the ass and smile, sure, can't see it any different…

(It was about 60 degrees and I was thinking flowers. Got off my ass. Took one train to another train to a third and did a little walking. Wound up at the Botanical Gardens.
Life!
Life was in bloom.
The rose bushes gave off an impression of underground knowledge.
They stayed rooted, stood rigid; it was as if they were waiting for
something that they knew was coming. Meanwhile,
the wildflowers danced with indifference; disenchanted with the globe,
they bent easy in the wind.
I thought the wildflowers were absolute madness.
I thought the wildflowers were absolute brilliance.
I had to ask myself:
How could they dance
and beam
with so much yellow
in the face of our future? And I had no answer. They weren't talking and I couldn't talk for them and so screw it. I had 600 bucks and an unquenchable thirst.)

Headed for an early death…

(I had 600 bucks and an unquenchable thirst. Stepped into a local bar and lost track of
Life!

Talked to a man
with a banker's nose and a shark grin. Gave the guy 60 bucks and he
gave me a square of tinfoil. I got into a stall of the men's room.
Unfolded the tinfoil.
Thing held a pile of white rocks.
I began beating at the rocks, pounding and hammering at them with
the bottom of a BIC lighter, breaking the rocks down into smaller
rocks, into pebbles, into gravel, into a silky fine powder,
rolled a dollar bill tightly and sniiiiiiffffft two giant lines for the
getaway, kick the heart into high gear as I speed off down Main St.) I
was headed somewhere…when I first started this thing (seems like
20 years gone past) I had the illusion of goals, objectives, thought I
saw a clear end (20 years gone past) and after speeding off down
Main St. twitching, jumpy, heart pumping, arms jerking, legs kicking
out in wild Tango spasms, a
pink fleshy convulsion moving at a hundred
and 86
thousand
miles per second, I realized that there's no clear end to anything
round this place, there's only movement, one motion leading into the
next and rivers, tributaries, trickles into reservoirs, tap water, urine,
evaporation, rain runs down the side of a hill and flows back
seamlessly, moving so damned fast (me) that I outran my body, lost
definition and became milky white, translucent, became an outline,
grew vague around the edges and then I was just a thought, just a
whisper of consciousness blazing through the mad chemical night…I
was
headed
somewhere…

INSIDE THE ACTOR'S STUDIO

She said something about the greatest tears
falling from the eyes of photographs…

And I whispered that the summer was close,
that we'd make it out alive…

She promised the impossible with a laugh,
and I told her that perseverance was the key.

She screamed
'The future has already been recorded!
What the hell can we ever hope to accomplish if we're trapped inside
of a photo?'

And I laughed
'It's only a matter of time.
One day, and soon, we'll get our hands around that damned
photographer's neck.'

She sighs,
and says it's all a hoax,
that we're all being fooled, that there's no such thing as time
or forward momentum, that there's only screwing, just one body
screwing another body and that body screwing the next and so on
down the line. Infinite ejaculate! We measure our progress in
orgasms,
and if it's a good screw,
well, then you're bound to come. Shit! Your history,
my history, all of history
is a hardcore pornography shoot. We're just bad actors
on a cheap set
and the director
has called in sick.

And I give her my best T.V. smile,
and grab her by the back of her neck,
and we hold that pose
as the cameras start to flash.

A CHOICE ENCOUNTER, A MOMENT OF ENLIGHTENMENT

ordered a beer
and sat down.
next to me was a mass of gray hair
and gray beard
some flesh
some blood
some bones
a few teeth.
guy opened up a hole in his face and puked out three words,
'burn it all'.
a brown bottle slammed down in front of me like some nose diving jetliner.
I looked at the big board and it flashed.
the big board flashed train departures and train arrivals,
track numbers
and destinations. I was in bar, I was in Penn Station, I was in New York,
with 20 minutes to kill.
the mass turned in my direction and puked all over my shirt,
'burn the trains, burn the commuters,
burn the busses, the subways, burn New York, L.A., Washington,
burn Alaska, burn it all'
I sucked at foam.
it bubbled up the bottle's neck and slid down the sides.
'burn the banks, burn the schools, burn the hospitals,
burn all the computers, microwaves, and wristwatches,
burn it all'
I drank half the beer.
my shirt was covered in puke and the big board flashed track 21.
'burn the police, burn the army, burn the national guard and the air force,

burn Time, burn the nine to five,
burn your family,
burn it all'
there was puke on my pants. it dribbled in chunks down my leg and splattered on my shoes.
I finished the beer.
5 minutes till take off,
still thirsty, New York,
sitting at a bar in Penn Station,
I signal the bartender for another round.
'burn Christmas, burn Valentines Day,
burn Hanukkah,
burn it all'
another jetliner crashed landed in front of me.
I was thinking of how the foam was like smoke,
the red label was fire,
all that golden liquid inside was the trapped souls of all the dead passengers and I was like some great mouthed god accepting them into my body.
'burn the telephone booths,
burn the automobile plants,
burn the jails, burn the supermarkets,
burn it all'
I was covered in puke.
people walked in and out of the bar but always in a circle around the puddle that had formed on the floor beneath me. my train was boarding on track 21, a bar in Penn Station, New York,
three words,
one thought,
'burn it all'.
I turned to the mass of gray hair
and gray beard,
the mass of some flesh and some blood and some bones,
the mass of few teeth,
and asked what he was drinking.
he lifted a short glass,

swished around the half a sip of liquor that sat at the bottom,
and puked,
'whiskey'.
I waved over the bartender,
ordered two glasses of whiskey,
and looked at the big board.
I had another 20 minutes to kill.

12 IN THE AFTERNOON

and the camera finds me
hanging round in front of Canterbury's (can't smoke inside, not
anymore) already half-cocked,
on beer since the a.m.
with this kid (poor fuck's enlisted in the Reserves, I think)
smoking rolled
and filtered
Turkish tobacco and the kid's mad to be stomping on quiet town
streets (kid would
trade it all in
for the desert
and the sweat) but right out front of Canterbury's is a bench
and that thing's positioned just right (sun and trees, birds, no
wind, that whole
tranquilized
summer feeling, warm air, the beach, barbecues, beer rolling in your
stomach and there's
no thoughts of allies or coalitions, robots, fruit flies or
deadlines,
timetables or schedules, just this bench,
that's it, and all you gotta do is sit on the thing, just sit) but
with the current state of affairs
the kid's not interested, he's dreaming of something
uh, a little more liberating,
a little more heroic
than all this and he finishes his smoke
and runs back inside the bar (they've got CNN in there,
they're televising the biggest damned reality show of all time
and I think it's real fucking scary) then a leaf shakes free from
one of the trees, a car drives by and honks twice at a young girl, I
get up and walk three blocks north,
for some reason,
I don't feel like going back inside.

IT DOESN'T GET ANY BETTER THAN THIS...

there's nothing else like it
being young
and drunk
and wandering the streets of Manhattan
with a dollar fifty in your pocket

it's almost enough

another twenty five cents
and you can buy a large can of beer to soften the train ride home
and while walking along Hudson
you start to cough
and you spit something out
something brown
green
something speckled with red and lighting a cigarette, you sit down on
the curb
and you study your handiwork
think
this is better than all the art that I've seen this year
maybe even in the last two years, but that's not true (last year you
were introduced
to a dead Russian in motel room
a dead Russian with vision
a dead Russian who saw the future and trapped it with paint, and you
may have never found out his name,
but that doesn't matter) and getting up off that curb
cutting across Harrison to make the 1/9 uptown
you stick your finger in every pay phone that you pass
get lucky
find a dime
two nickels
a few scattered pennies

it's enough

you make Penn Station
and head for the beer vendor…

"Hello Mr. John!"
"Hey Ali, how's it going?"
"Very good today, very good. How are you Mr. John?"
"Ali, today, today I feel beautiful."
"Mr. John…"
"Yes Ali?"
"You look beautiful today, there is a light in your eyes." and he looks embarrassed, puts his head down and holds out the beer "Here Mr. John, no charge."
"Thank you Ali." dumping my change into the tip jar "Take care of yourself. I'll see you tomorrow."

and on the train ride home
reading Hemingway
Dostoevsky
Castaneda
Burroughs
sucking on a tall can of beer
watching the lights and the stores and the people zip by
you think to yourself
I hope it never changes
I hope it always stays this way
just being young
and drunk
and wandering the streets of Manhattan
with a dollar fifty in my pocket

3 AM WAITING

on one line, one word, one
anything. Meanwhile,
outside,
there's something hanging round
there's something painting the walls
there's something grinning at the window
and laughing loud in the rain.
It's always that damned rain.
Damned rain will make you feel like the fall-apart kid,
a few flashes of poetry
and then disappearing
into the milk easy night.
You drop so simple, while
waiting on brilliance
to knock down your door
to grab you by the shirt collar and pin you to the machine. Mean-
while,
inside,
there's something stuck
there's something stuck between a rock
there's something stuck between a rock and a hard place and that
something is you, damned
fall- apart kid
with your few flashes of poetry
and your milk easy night. Question: What're you going to do
when the brilliance doesn't come? When that one line, one word, one
anything doesn't come? Answer: The only thing that you can do.
Type something like this
and
wait.

GOOD LUCK, HALF-HEART

flyby night in an easy town
there're eyes in the corridor, whispers of magnetic funerals,
draws metallic participants from across the globe, there're memories of forbidden afternoons
and a high gloss escape out a second story window, memories of a young man
working on flowers and immortality,
half heart fed his resolve to the birds and kept the bread for himself, didn't understand
takes a certain amount of strength to play this game,
takes a certain amount of backbone that he just doesn't have, young man wants to turn the plane around, runs up the aisle
only to realize that the cockpit's been locked,
and the pilot gone missing,
realizes that he's just another passenger
and that all the passengers are scared, good luck
half heart,
you're gonna need it

THE MUSICIAN

Up since 11
snorting Norcos and drinking beer.
Up since 11 snorting- I should be working on the novel,
I should be pressuring Leon the editor to get out the second collection,
I should be
snorting Norcos and drink beer and saying screw it, let it take care of itself while I
play the keyboard like a piano, while the mind goes numb and the eyes slide shut,
screw it, I'm a sponsored man,
thanks to this keyboard and a good friend (I've been running 12 hrs
like this, jumping between the guitar and the computer (looking at
porn (you just have to)), opening veins. the whole bit, to post
another…shit, I can't even call this poetry; it's a half a case of beer
and a nose full of white
playing the keyboard like a piano) - I should be discussing chapbooks with Renee,
I should be submitting to an Indian anthology, I should be doing any and every
thing
that deals with
snorting more Norcos
and drinking more beer and playing this keyboard
as if it were a piano.

THAT MESS ON THE SIDEWALK

There's something warped, wrapped up in love
that allows a man
to hate his woman
and vice-versa, yelling, foaming like
mad dogs,
and hands reaching out
to strangle the young lover…

There's something twisted, intertwined with love
that drives cars over cliffs,
and trunk over hood, a tumbling eternity,
hands reaching across the seat
in search of the young lover…

There's something so crazy,
so intense,
something so wild and compelling, there's
something that throws knives at the young lover's heart, there's
something that tosses axes from across the room, there's
something that trips, stumbles, pushes and sends
the young lover off the balcony…

(screaming 5 flights of affection)

Watching the young lovers from a window, there's
something
so human
about it all.

IT WAS IN A 45

dollar a night screw shack (place was full of hermaphrodites, pimps,
assassins and transients) somewhere around upstate New York,
sitting Indian style on a bed (thing was mess of fleas, mites, blood
stains, lice crabs and dandruff flakes) with the infamous blonde
and
we we're half-drunk
off a case of cheap domestic (a mixed, processed, carbonated and
bottled golden liquid
fit only for the palates of the most noble of rednecks and
backwoodsmen) playing cards
at 2 a.m.
and grateful
for our escape- we had beat the masses; the murderers, the vampires,
the electronic Japanese kids that crawl and buzz through downtown
Manhattan like robotic fruit flies with slicked black hair- and their
hair isn't even hair, it's ultra thin strands of fiber optic wires and
receptors and transmitters, recording sound and image, recording
taste, feel and smell, recording your movements, my movements,
your parent's movements, recording taxi cabs and sex shops and
book vendors, these wires suck up every bit of that precious informa-
tion and dump it all into some central intelligent processing robotic
fruit fly decision making unit which comes up with theories, predic-
tions, classifications, calculations of speeds and distances, mapping
out plans of action and thought patterns, deducing trajectories, orbits,
ETA'S and STD'S then compiling, encrypting and broadcasting
indecipherable messages to some mother ship that's hovering above
Manhattan, maybe over by the Seaport somewhere, yeah (area's a
magnet for ET's,
ship jumpers, immigrants,
fruit flies and refugees) and we had beat them all,
started the car and moved North until the landscape became snow
capped mountains and small diners

by the side of the road, just a little getaway from the concrete/steel/
red brick lifestyle that we'd trapped ourselves into,
and retreating to this motel,
this little safe haven, somewhere
around upstate New York, enclosed
by 4 rented walls and the wolves kept at bay,
the silent phone,
a t.v. sits in the background,
we
dead bolted the door and stripped down to nothing,
took a bucket of ice
and beer
and hopped under the warm spray of the shower head…

it was in a 45
dollar a night screw shack, somewhere
around upstate New York…and it was perfect

ONE FOR THE ANALYSTS, ONE FOR THE EXAMINERS, ONE FOR THE SCRUTINIZERS AND PICK-APART ARTISTS

I've replaced the Combine with the Machine (Kesey)
swinging from the rafters (line's reminiscent of Burroughs)
smell of death on her neck like a perfume (Ernie screams through the decades
'You fucking thief!')
metallic twilight
of night's
shiny steal neon glow (sends Kerouac into a frenzy)
the most charming of cunts, teased my balls with her tongue, I
emptied two pints down her throat and waltzed out onto Mercer
(Miller shakes his head)
that money chin line
from 'The Reading' (Fitzgerald raises an eyebrow)
scotch-whiskey while tracing a rhinoceros in the cracks of my ceiling (Hank
sneers,
guy's beneath six feet of dirt
and stronger than ever)
I borrowed the beat from another John (Frusciante in Amsterdam)
the bouncing, rolling, floating on the barge dream with the typewriter
jumping, leaving indents on the table (hey Tommy!)
'It started at my feet. Sucking up the smoke and where my feet once
were I saw an empty space, my feet were in the smoke and the smoke
was in the seagull and I began to realize what was happening. The
smoke was coming off my legs now and the seagull inhaled it and my
legs disappeared, and then my thighs, and then my torso,
and then my chest was gone
and I was only a head
covered in smoke
and then I was only the smoke

and then I was inside of the seagull...' (in there I met Castaneda)
a long sleeve, collared shirt of double fold Egyptian cotton and a pair
of hand-crafted, box-toed shoes made from the softest chocolate
brown leather in all of Italy (a gift from Ian)
"I might be going to hell in a bucket baby…." (Garcia)
and
BIG CAPITAL LETTERS
WILL REMIND YOU (of McCullers)
take the whole jumbled mess,
toss in two grams of coke and a prescription of valium, codeine,
xanax, oxy-contin, a couple of the yellow
714mg
lemon drop
quaaludes,
a job in downtown Manhattan, no concept of a tomorrow,
a canister of Dust-off,
a large bottle of Dewars and a cheap case of domestic,
some long blonde hair
to tie it all up…(and you've got a Dempsey poem, enjoy
fuckers)

- THE SEA
- RIVERS AND BRIDGES
- MOUNTAINS
- NIGHT ON THE EARTH
- THINGS WITHIN A HOUSE
- GREEN TEA
- DRINKING
- SPORTING AND PLAYING THINGS
- WOMEN AND YOUNG GIRLS
- A GIRL'S TRUE LOVE
- SINCERE LOVE
- PASSIONATE LOVE
- SORROWFUL LOVE
- GODS AND BUDDHA
- BUDDHA'S LOVE

By Kazuyosi Ikeda

THE SEA

Lo, white and deep blue compose a fine striped pattern.
The midsummer's sea assumes a deep blue colour.
The foaming waves, forming stripes, are white like silver.
Nature makes a beauteous, exquisite pattern.

How beauteous the scenes of this inland sea are !
Seen are islets near by and the other land far.
They appear and are hidden at evening misty.
Do I See a vision or a reality ?

In the seaside village there's a sea breeze blowing.
I roam around aimlessly in ragged clothing.
The lone sky is not easy to get dark early.
I hear a plover alone call his friend fondly

When the tide is coming in, the sea waves boom out;
In powerful deep voices the waves are roaring.
All things in heaven and earth are now prospering.
Listen, in this mighty sea all things' lives cry out.

I, a marker buoy, float on the waves all day,
To tell the ships sincerely their accurate way.
Every night I, looking up at starry heaven,
Sleep on my dear sea, my roost peaceful and open.

What time will my life be snatched very cruelly
By the deep raving fiercely and violently ?
Every night I, the captain, look up at sad stars,
To see by astrology my fate from the stars.

RIVERS AND BRIDGES

Into a ravine's bottom have I strayed deeply.
Alas, losing my bearings, I'm solitary.
I've found a stream; my thirst is slaked by its water.
The staff of young life ! precious is the stream's water.

In this riverside district I enjoy my life.
Clean water in this river purifies my life.
My hear is limpid, looking at lucid water.
Dreams arise from my heart touched with gracious water.

I cross a ditch by a bridge with casualness.
Halfway crossing, I look down at the dirty ditch.
Of a sorrowful colour is the unclean ditch.
I think about my own life of great filthiness.

O the bridge of rigid stone is firm and steady.
On it I walk with sure step strongly in safety.
Fine and lucid are the waves of the spring river.
The water under the bridge sings with voice tender.

The crude, poor suspension bridge oover the ravine
Is swaying by the strong wind; ah, the deep ravine !
My feet, while crossing the bridge, cower by horror.
Quiet darkness of the depths contains great danger.

I float on water and rock on the worldly waves.
I am trodden by men's feet every day sadly.
I am a vain floating bridge, unsure and dreamy;
I sob and weep bitterly, wet through with the waves.

MOUNTAINS

I am much alone here deep in the mountain's heart.
I've strayed into a strange place: ah ! i've lost my way.
Yearning for men in this world, I shout from my heart ;
Echoes sound loudly and spread wide and far away.

Distressed by love, I ascend the summer mountain.
Amidst a thick growth of trees, I stray aimlessly.
I think I hear the neighing of a horse surely.
No, I hear a robin's song, feeling grief-stricken.

A gallant man in a cap and dress for hunting
Enters the mountain to kill birds in life joyous.
A pretty young bird is short by his skilled firing ;
A pine gets wet with the blood of the bird grievous.

We tread on the mountain way, whitely glistening.
Our held pickels are our swords, the souls of climbers.
The snowy mountain, lofty, steep and outstanding,
Of sublime azure colour, with great hope, glitters.

The breasts of the mountains are genial and tender.
The depths of the forests are truehearted and green.
The sky is pure and clear and clouds are white and clean.
The mountain village : the place quiet for ever !

The plants on me, a mountain, have died completely.
How ugly my figure is ! ah, what shamefulness !
My naked skin is exposed to bitter coldness;
I shiver, the winter wind blowing heavily.

NIGHT ON THE EARTH

I am helpless and lonely; now right has fallen.
I long for the ume trees aeen in the garden.
Being there, I only smell the fragrant blossoms.
Meanwhile the bright moon rises, lighting the blossoms.

The beach wind blows bracingly in the summer night.
While petals of a crinum sway enchantingly.
Pieces of pure-white cloth float and drift dreamily,
Tastefully and wondrously in the dark of night.

Tonight in winter it's cold; the monlight's chilly.
A night heron is standing by the pond stilly.
I recollect my lover, when looking at it.
Ah, he, while still alive, was as noble as it.

I wish to see her at night amorous in spring.
Near her I draw, obstructed by a screen of cloth.
Blown by the night breeze, it is shaking and swaying.
I'm before the hanging screen of pink floral cloth.

At night the light of the street glimmers gloomily.
Now in winter the light soaks in the eyes coldly.
A weary traveler walks, making a shadow.
Severe sadness is contained deep in the shadow.

Men's eyes see not any things in the dark of night ;
So the night eyes are grievous unlimitedly.
The shadows seen are graceful in the dark of night ;
So the night eyes are joyous unlimitedly.

THINGS WITHIN A HOUSE

This scar on the writing desk I used long ago
Is a trace of my scratching of immense sorrow
While writing a love letter not acceptable.
Ah, a vestige of my grief extinguishable.

A girl, with hair black, long, lithe, naps on a sofa.
At first she thought of sleeping only transiently.
Before long in the dreamland she wanders sweetly,
Without knowing how her skirt is in disorder.

We made efforts very hard on a winter's day.
We have now time of quiet in this living room.
The scent of tea we drink drifts all over the room.
Our warm hearts are united in a sincere way.

Through the round window we see the sky in round shape.
It's a mysterious sphere lapis lazuli,
Enveloping white clear clouds roundly and gently.
In the dreamland do we see a gem in round shape ?

In this calm and still study I'm alone sitting.
I'm besieged by many books very heavily.
My heart, expanded, wanders unlimitedly.
I zealously wish to write poems enchanting.

Shoes, boots, sandals, and wood clogs! You walked hard today.
On extremely trying ways you walked the whole day.
So tired, you may repose and make yourselves easy.
This old footgear cupboard is your lodging happy.

GREEN TEA

I make tea from powdered tea and drink it calmly.
Chrysanthemums are fragrant in my hermitage.
The mountain's depths are unchanged everlastingly.
Peacefulness of my heart is utmost advantage.

My small tea room is flooded with mood of autumn.
I've a tea ceremony for hearts' brief stillness
To taste my floavourful tea, my good friends have come.
The tea's relish is supreme; here's great happiness.

The tea ceremony gets our hearts linked tightly.
We gently drink, passing round, a cup of strong tea.
We feel the cup's heaviness and the taste of tea.
We have a marvellous feast in this world stilly.

Powdered green tea is contained in the small caddy.
During the night of autumn it may sleep calmly.
I, early in the morning, open the caddy.
The lapis lazuli sky is limpid greatly.

I scoop up powdered green tea with the special spoon.
With my heart very quiet, on a spring morning.
The Japanese spirit, too, I scoop with the spoon.
The powdered green tea spoon has strength fascinating.

In the cup I put weak tea, powdered minutely.
Its green colour is as light as departed dreams.
Hot water put, with the whisk, I make tea foamy.
The foam is lively and fresh just as spring's sweet dreams.

DRINKING

To men in this mundane world trying severely,
Refined saké is good food for vitality.
It soaks keenly in the depth of human belly ;
Men's dreams expand vastly and glitter brilliantly.

I alone warm the bottle containing saké,
As if I warmed my small dream, the night deepening.
Thinking keenly of the world's merciful feeling,
From the bottle to a cup I pour warm saké.

My friend and I understand each other truly,
This evening, offering and accepting a cup
Filled with saké containing cordial thoughts deeply.
I drink saké mixed with tears of his from the cup.

The light is poor and gloomy on a winter's night.
Unrefined saké do we, two, drink together.
Our dreams by the fireside are very warm tonight.
The songs crooned by us enchant deeply each other.

I am a saké barrel, with hoops gripping plates.
With stomach full of saké, I get drunk madly,
So the hoops' loosening makes gaps between the plates.
Drops of saké are dripping through the gaps grossly.

Vodka is the strongest drink, as strong as the fire
Of a young girl's heart burning in worldly darkness.
Drunk with such strong alcohol, I sleep with deepness ;
I rely on drink to make my sorrow expire.

SPORTING AND PLAYING THINGS

In the shade of trees covered with flowers scarlet,
This morn my friend plays tennis with a fine racket.
The white ball does he return strongly and firmly.
Upon his arms do flowers fall elegantly.

The girl ! slide hard on the ice ! the girl in the skates !
That's the New Year's first skating with thy great pleasure.
Skate lightly with happy smile, in thy fine ice skates,
Sliding, jumping and spinning, with thy sweet figure !

I made a resolve to vault that big vaulting horse.
The way of a man's mind is blocked up by that horse.
Ahead of a man it stands so impudently.
If I vault it, my mind will get clear perfectly.

Glass beads, named marbles, run straight swiftly on the ground .
The tiny boys' hearts leap up with extreme pleasure.
In the play the friends compete with one anohter.
Like the round beads, the boys' souls brighten and are round.

A dear little girl alone does the taw playing.
Like petals and stars, the taws is she filliping.
They are of colours yellow, red and blue deeply.
Her dreams enlarge boundlessly and shine brilliantly.

Catching and throwing up bags, a loveable girl
Is playing beanbags deftly with her hands pretty.
Whose daughter on earth is she ? Let her be happy !
With hair hanging down the back, the dear little girl !

WOMEN AND YOUNG GIRLS

A roundly living woman with a round chignon !
She wanders around this world, unsafe, clamorous,
Transmigrating like a wheel whirling on and on.
Her behaviour is luscious, sweet and beauteous.

Ah, tonight, the woman is very amorous !
The perfume is fragrant and feels voluptuous.
It penetrates from her skin, graceful and tender,
Through her extremely thin clothes of a pink colour.

I gaze with zeal on my face in a hand mirror.
I feel my image to be supremely lovely.
It's natural that people admire my beauty.
Of my own face I become fonder and fonder.

Day by day growing, ardent and vehement love
Has caused the dishevelment of my raven hair !
With care, with the boxwood comb, I'm combing my hair,
Resolving to let none know my deep hidden love.

A girl's hair hangs down the back sleekly and lithely.
This morn, she's lost deep in thought : her hair is straggly.
Her tender and fragile breast shakes with emotion.
Fiery love increases her heart's confusion.

A pretty girl's hair is cut even and straightly.
Red floral ornaments put on her raven hair
Seem to be somewhat modest on her short bobbed hair.
The flowers nearly drop down sadly and finely.

A GIRL'S TRUE LOVE

White is the heart of a girl innocent of love.
As a white hydrangea turns its colour to red,
So the happy girl soon falls in passionate love
And with her life flaming up, her heart becomes red.

The red brooch on a girl's breast is very dazzling.
Amply bathed with the sunlight shed glitteringly,
The brooch shines like the girl's heart flaming intensely
Out of so passionate love that her blood's seething.

A pretty loveable girl, with lips red deeply !
Her blood , as red as her lips, is burning briskly :
Enraptured with love, she pines for her beloved.
Her crimson lips, thickly rouged, are brightly lighted.

Drawn in the picture postcard are flowers gorgeous.
They are in bloom in purple, red and pink colour.
My hand written on the back is faint and slender,
Conveying to my lover my heart so zealous.

Beat the hand drum in the path of darkness of love !
Beat off the pent-up anger of tragical love !
Beat down the heartless, cold man hard and terribly !
The black hair is dishevelled and unkempt harshly.

Alas ! as iron is hard, so his heart is hard.
As iron sinks in water, his heart is gloomy.
Ah ! with on iron hammer, my heart he hits hard ;
Sadly, he shatters my dream of love utterly.

SINCERE LOVE

The scene on the pond evokes profound emotion.
Watch the two mandarin ducks who love each other.
They always swim together, with deep affection.
On the brave male the female attends for ever.

Thou art the great and deep sea ; I'm a fishing net.
Night after night I plunge down into thee deeply,
So that I may catch the fish in thee entirely,
Because the fish are thy heart, profound and secret.

Putting on a soft hat deep, I walk on the way ;
The trees' leaves fall lonesomely, on an autumn day.
A few fallen leaves are put on my soft hat's brim.
Ardent love for the girl fills my brain to the brim.

My heart is an iron nail, firm and straightforward.
The fine girl ! I will attain my desire inward.
By driving the nail straightly, I will win thy heart.
The nail, my heart, shall firmly pierce thee to the heart.

I will pack in a parcel my heart filled with love.
To my lover in the town I'll post it fondly.
In the country the sea's dark ; I languish with love.
About the far town's heaven I think ardently.

Strong are spiritual bonds between thee and me.
There is a deep destiny linking thee and me.
Ah, thy heart and my heart are fastened with a clamp.
Even death can't sever us ; so firm is the clamp.

PASSIONATE LOVE

O a black cat caterwauls on an autumn night.
In the sky the full moon is glorious and bright.
The cat's eyes shine glaringly and fierily :
With passionate love his heart flames vehemently.

Thou and I are kingfishers : thou art my sweetheart.
Take the fish held in my bill ; I caught it for thee.
My passionate love for thee is firing my heart.
And making my blue wings shake to a slight degree.

How painful is the nail thrust deep into my heart !
Every day incessantly it tortures my heart.
Ah ! it is the nail of love I can not pull out.
My beloved ! with pincers, pull thou the nail out !

My love ! thou hast included thy heart in this box.
The heart kept secret, I try to unlock the box.
My fingers, to put the key into the keyhole,
Tremble more and more as they approach the keyhole.

Shedding tears by pungency of curry powder,
I soak myself in yearning for thee, my sweetheart.
Thy pure, moist and golden skin never leaves my heart.
It is like curry powder kneaded with water.

The letters from my sweetheart increase in number.
Her burning love penetrates my bosom deeply.
Pretty letters are piled up higher and higher.
To strengthen love in my breast, I'll file them tightly.

SORROWFUL LOVE

The sands are full of a mood dark and piteous.
Having parted from my love, I trudge on the sands.
The sands on which I tread weep in a voice grievous.
My sorrow is much deepened by the weeping sands.

Heard is a cry for yearning after the sweetheart.
A Japanese bellflower, light purple, opened.
The cry heard is its bell's ring all around broadened.
The bell in the autumn field rings in a man's heart.

In love with her, my heart's pains are piled complexly.
A tortoise-shell pattern is the shape of my heart.
The shape is vividly seen with reality,
And so tortures severely the core of my heart.

I pick flowers and put them into the basket.
To my lover I'll send it with my grievous love.
Ah, a conveyer of love ! the flower basket
Full of the colours of love and the scents of love !

My pen for my love letter, lying in the case,
Waits with zeal to be taken out for use from the case.
But I'll keep my pen of love in the case firmly,
And I'll hide my dream of love in my breast deeply.

Standing on tiptoe, I see the leaving man off.
The sight of his back departs from me and goes off.
I shall not see him again, but my hot heart's fire,
Which flamed up fiercely last night, will never expire.

GODS AND BUDDHA

This mundane world is flooded with sorrowful tears.
For not abandoning me I truly pray Gods.
Worshipping Gods' shelf, I add a few of my tears.
To the sacred tree branches offered for the Gods.

Not knowing what I should do, I come to the shrine.
When drawing a sacred lot, my hand shakes slightly.
The heavens without clouds and the glorious shrine
Are still and calm and all is peaceful perfectly.

The strong divine spirit now comes out graciously,
Upon the portable shrine carried devoutly,
Onto the streets of the town this blissful evening.
There gather a huge crowd of people adoring.

The temple stands in the depths of the high mountain,
Far from worldly pollution, and near to Heaven.
The utmost Buddhist truth is studied here deeply.
Descending of Buddha's soul is seen vividly.

In this street many temples stand venerably.
Buddha's holy paradise do they well create.
Here and there white jasmines are in bloom fragrantly.
Ah, an everlasting bliss do they celebrate !

The sound of a wood-block drum is heard lonesomely.
The sound echoes in the skies growing dark slowly.
A priest, unknown, is chanting a Buddhist sutra.
Every night we hear the voice solemn and sober.

BUDDHA'S LOVE

The surface of the pond is full of lotuses.
Heart-clearing ! the white flowers of the lotuses !
On one of their calyxes, I see distinctly,
Today too, the Buddha's shape, holy and lofty.

O high in the night sky, huge colourful curtains !
Aurorae, surprising us in the camping ground !
We see Buddha descending from heaven to ground,
Wrapped in the magnificent, glittering curtains.

All the young and old people in this mundane land !
Recognize the great merits of Buddhist sutras !
Read them ! Then from Heaven come Buddha's followers
To take you to the holy, glittery dreamland.

In the west sky I'm looking at the sickle moon ;
Its silver colour's solemn and mysterious.
I feel my heart is allured by the noble moon
To Buddha's far-off west land, holy and gracious.

My body is smeared with mud : My heart is muddy.
The full moon brilliantly shines on my soiled body.
I will leave my filthy stain and vicious offence
To Buddha's holy moonlight of intelligence.

Forsaking the mundane world, women serve Buddha.
In the nun temple they pray with rosary beads.
Holy, sublime music drifts from their counted beads.
The music of the next world governed by Buddha !

- THE EASTER ARSONIST
- WITH BATED BREATH
- SECOND HAND MADNESS
- THIS WICKED LIFE
- CAPTURED IN MID FLIGHT
- DWELLING
- INEVITABLE
- VIOLENTANGO
- UNPRONOUNCEABLE GREASY STUFF
- TRAGIC WALTZ
- TWILIGHT ECHO
- WEAK
- JUST A BAD IDEA
- MAKING FACES
- END OF THE ROPE

By Richard Conrad Henry

THE EASTER ARSONIST

I think I should be thankful
for all those
itshouldbecheese &
wishwasham sadwiches
for all the agnostic
roundabout foreing beers
the psychic wines
and juices of delightful berries
the forget-me-not meats displayed
askance
all turning and jumping in a total
kitchen frenzy
and be also thankful
to those who go barking mad
in the howling wind
and shut their eyes
in the shadow
of a
shivering.

WITH BATED BREATH

Promising nightfall
at 10 pm
tha sky looks like
the roaring 20's
from a lost and found hotel balcony
in the middle of July
with a ghost of a chance
of sobering up
and a munched cigarette
dangling from unshaven jaws
the city air
smells of progress
of multi-racial cookery
of whores displayed in aspic
standing in broken doorways
looking like dead hedgehogs
and
there's no beergut
large enough to match
my thirst
nor
gutter dark & filthy enough
to drown my hands into
this roach room
that fills with my screams
of drunken lonely moments
look......Death's beaconing
from different angles
Fear twitches my fingertips
as Silence approaches.

SECOND HAND MADNESS

Not carefully
chosen words
but thoughts
pinned on the wall
chase venomous
spiders of broken
destiny
as the dust keeps
blowing upwards
covering my desk
and every damned thing
on it
uncorking the red
in a fog of
telephone ringings
stuck in the unforgiving
game
of forced patience
waiting for Godot or
acceptance
or something good
to happen
I stare at the
hairy crotch of
Insanity
licking my lips
like a thirsty dog.

THIS WICKED LIFE

I'm in the dark
in stereo delight
walking through
flames of shining
desires
drinking slowly from
melting cups
the toxic lucidity
of mouring
of self-pity
and disgrace
chewing the bitter
seed of stupidity
over & over again
I'm in a vortex
in velvet tenderness
ripping open old wounds
to feel the pain
to hurt again
and see if it was
worth it, afterall
sometimes the older
you get the more
you remember
(unless you're forced
to forget)
and
if orgasm
is the pleasure
of creation
then
Madness
must be
the bliss
of DECAY.

CAPTURED IN MID FLIGHT

Behind mirrors
stealing images
you create the fire
I must feed
every single day
behind curtains
whispering suggestions
you fabricate a world
I must breach
somehow, someway
I'm stuck between
a waterfall of
frozen bad ideas
and the sinking feeling
of losing all this time
chasing after the unreal.

DWELLING

I fish in the shallows
of daylight
and use my old dreams
as a bait
I dip in the lukewarm pond
of exuberance
reminding myself
not to panic
the water boils with
all of my torments
and fools around
with my faith
I know that somewhere
salvation awaits me
as I sink deeply
in the foam
of a tragedy
and the slime at the bottom
invites me to stay
as the crabs munch
at my sorrow
and the stream
whispers my name.

INEVITABLE

Exhilarant terror
grabs the legs
of the kitchen table
as I flex my imagination
to fit every curve
of the body
intense &
swaying
like
the instability
of a soft drink
big monkey laughter
explodes &
shatters my lips
as I flex
my imagination
some more
and the body
melts and drips
on night time's ashes
evening's dishes
afternoon's groceries
and morning's wishes
intense
& bubbling
like
the purity
of a glass of water
grotesque fright
hugs the
refrigerator
as I loosen up,

releasing the images
that fit every
curve
of the body
immense
& razor sharp
like
the iniquity
of a strong drink
the body swells
back to normal
sucking from
dawn's tits
the right amount of alcohol
and passes out.

VIOLENTANGO

Pre-heated
bandoneon sadness
squatting on nobody's
innocence
riding nobody's care
sultry & reckless
up and down the scales
reptile endurance
waiting in the darkness
liquor thick & unnerving
like a small hours promise
lukewarm sax despair
sliding from nobody's heart
trembling like an autumn leaf
shining on the dark side
of the spoon
diamondback fear
rushing out way too soon
twirling in dirty sheets
marinated in scotch
with a hint of halitosis
I regain my senses
when it's almost
dawning.

UNPRONOUNCEABLE GREASY STUFF

Graphic &
explicit hunger
for a slim chance
of survival
ancient & recent
history revolving
on itself
flasks filled
with pregnant clouds
overflowing
with glowing nights
with burning lights
and pungent pain
"just give this poor man
another glass of rain"
detailed &
focused thirst
for a small chance
of getting away with it
present & more recent
history
spinning
on its axis
basins filled
with delivering clouds
(dark and bloody
just like the 20th century)
overflowing
with burning nights
with glowing lights
with the killers
& the insane

"just pour this poor man
another glass of rain"
pre-recorded &
staged fear
of having missed the point
of staying out of it
now's the time
and now alone
oceans filled
with afterbirth
(bloody and dark
like the beginning of this century)
overflowing
with the flames
with the screams
with the slashed veins
"and don't forget to make him
pay...........
for that last glass
of rain".

TRAGIC WALTZ

Beneath this superb sky
lies the funnel of Time
behind this excellent moon
sleeps the corkscrew of Life
beyond this pretty soup bowl
hangs the ladle of Death
before this extravagant person
swings the cleaver of Boredom
as vaguely seen from a mirror
an obese shadow.

TWILIGHT ECHO

The razor miaows
on the table top
killing and buying
time
when the phone
barks at my tree
at 1 am
emptying the
graveyard shift's
ashtrays
I'm suspended
in tight-ass
seclusion
imbibed in
damaging spirits
& rattlesnake
sweetness
I'm defying the laws
of cyber flaws
of frantic delusions
unable to shine
through the shadows.

WEAK

This is the serious
side of night
with camouflage kisses
& red eyes
burning with
insomnia
jousting with bottle/weed
growling at the
blank pages
last minute doubts
killing the lines
prematurely
this is the strong
side of night
with overall whispers
& white knuckles
trembling in anguish
gambling on luck/genius
cursing the
empty scrapbook
indecision(fast-foreward)
drowning all of
the ideas
'write about what you know'
(one of the rules for those with
NO fantasy)
this is a
brutal mistake
I work harder
than ever
but the gods
stand in the darkness
laughing their asses
off.

JUST A BAD IDEA

Stretching against
the wall of
this switchblade night
all spiced up and crunchy
in the takeaway kitchen
of a smile
I'm no tourist in Sin City
got my own damn place to stay
just like a scarecrow in Cuban heels
dressed up in pure elation
too many shadows across my face.

MAKING FACES

Crushed teeth
in pearly white ice
fitting nicely
in the glass trap
wet with poison
split lips
on translucent borders
aching loudly
in semi darkness
clumsy tongue
uncurling briefly
with viscous speed
numb with needle stings
sore throat
in red membranes
with jolts & spasms
drenched in
bad libation
"Puah!
I'm NEVER gonna
touch this stuff
again!"
I says
putting down
the longdrink
glass.

END OF THE ROPE

Tonight
I haven't got
anything for you
not one thought
not one useful line
there's nothing under the
carpet
no skeleton in the closet
left unturned
not a crumb of prejudice
not a whisper of contradiction
not even a shred of gossip
tonight the horizon
doesn't sparkle
the squares are empty
there's not a soul
in sight
(including mine)
and yet
silence dies
a sweet death
by the chokehold harmony of
a piano concerto
(the Rach 3)
and watching beauty
becoming a killer too
it lacerates every bit of hope
I had left.

By Serge van Duijnhoven

COFFEE

I was four and fell with my scooter
down the stairs with the marble tiles
at home in the sitting room and I fell
hard and with my head back to front on
the tiles and I screamed and Mum saw that
blood was flowing from my head and
Mum screamed and I screamed and Mum ran
into the street to get help and it
was still hurting and our Egyptian
neighbor opposite knew how to make
the pain go away she said she knew the cure
she said that was with coffee from the
coffee package she said and she rubbed the
coffee into the dark hole on my head
and I felt the sting of the coffee
in my entire head and in my body
and it still hurt a great deal and
since then I never drink coffee
and I hardly sleep

from: *Copycat* (Prometheus, 1996)

HOMEWARD BOUND

All strangers are born as children of their families
All strangers have played in houses they called home
On est tous des étrangers. Travellers coming round
wandering through a space that everybody
has to confisquate. But where there's a will
there's a way. Stubborness is what drives us all
and drives us crazy. To live fully from the land
the soil in which the seeds are spread with the hand.
The hair on our heads is as the cane on our roofs.
Our cracked skin is as the eroded walls of our shags.
Transparency is the scare of our bones. Our voice cries
at best for help. What we are seeking is rest.
Asilum in eternity. What we are is where we have been
falling: cerebral hunters and hunted prey.
We are game in the woods. A hungry flock in nature's
hungry mouth. We are obedient and futile. Tiny
particles floating around. Our names have been assigned
and even the gift of life was not our choice.
Every single good we own and everything we are
is borrowed, shareware, bonds and loans. Property
of Time alone; that vicious, greedy stockbroker
and billionaire, who having been born without a soul
supports no other soul as company. Who has no friends
or relatives, and rules the earth
as if he were the master of the universe.
We owe him all - as he insists - and everybody has to pay.
His will is merciless. No exceptions, no delays.
Who prays for help, will be harrassed.
Who disobeys, will disappear. He holds us hostage
Nobody is free to stay. We have to leave and
sneak out like thieves. When evening comes
we pack our bags. We cross the border
in the thick of night. Our exitpapers are called:
death.

---

from: *The Golden Wings; an anthology of world poetry* (India 2002)

CHRISTIAN LOIDL

1957 (Linz) – 2001 (Vienna)

I
Open
The
Door

The
Door
Opens
Me

MORTU TOMBU MIYI

'Mortu tombu miyi', the title of the following poem = a vernacular saying in Haiti, meaning: all things buried and gone. It was the title of a specific cycle of poems from Falsche Prophezeiungen, a magnificent book written by the Austrian poet Christian Loidl, who died in December 2001 at the age of 44 after tragically falling out of a window in his Viennese apartment – a death similar to the one of Bohumil Hrabal, the Czech writer he highly respected. Hrabal seemingly fell down while trying to spot a blackbird that was singing underneath his hospital window. Chris – just before tumbling towards his death - also must have been enchanted by the luring song of some dark bird that waited to get out of its cage and 'melt with the air'.

In some way, it feels as if Chris fulfilled the crystal-clear imperative uttered by the enlightened voice that enchantedly rises up at the end of his last book of poetry: *Kleinstkompetenzen; Erinnerungen aus einer geheimen Kindheit*: 'Luft musst mann sein… Luft musst mann sein (...)' - in English: 'Air is what we should be… Air is what we should be'. The day before the accident, Chris had sent me a message that he had changed his email address into 'airpoet@.gmx.at'. The symbolic meaning of this I only understood weeks later, when I visited Vienna to take part in the memorial-night organised by his close friends and allies. After having climbed up the sandstone stairs of the building in the Vereinsgasse (II Bezirk) where Christian lived, my eyes fell on a little blue metal plate that was attached to the frontdoor of the deserted apartment that I knew quite well, saying: 'airpoet'. It was a souvenir Chris had taken home from one of his travels in Lithuania, where this magical word simply means 'airport'. Suddenly, it all clicked and became clear, and I realised that my friend indeed must have melted with the air he aspired so wisely and breathed so deeply.

The laserbeam in front of the night-club
touches the sky in search of God
all air blows away

the moon stands high
as a tiny fingerprint
in the stained window
of heaven

We see more
talk less
thunder in the far land
of our memory
water, drops, mud
rain is still more clear
than blood

To live is to retreat
a ritual of goodbyes
a wounding in slow-motion
the ailment of addiction
our dreams fade away
like fog in the morning
our beloved ones depart
what we cherish, perishes
what we leave behind is the pain
to go beyond is to be healed

To bear the chain, you said
one has to sing - because
air is the important thing
the air is always young
the air wears no grey hair
the air never ends up in a wheelchair
Luft müsst mann sein
Luft müsst mann sein
Nicht mehr so mühd
Nicht mehr so mühd
Wach müsst mann sein

---

from: *Bloedtest* (De Bezige Bij, album + cd coming up in 2003)

PINKFINGERED ROSES

feel with your fingers
the tender, night-buttoned bodies
taste with your tongue the anchovis
filled with little grains of heroine
fix out your wrinkles
before it gets crawling under your skin

rehydrate the music, the concertos
of feeble vibrations
undo with the idols
of current generations
wrap up all the leftovers
of lost inspiration

have an eye on the rest
and take care of the dangers
beware of all hazards, of pity
and scorn, insurance agents
of women and strangers

suck out the fat in all levels
of your mind, undress yourself
from the notion of time
cut the cables of emotions
intertwine all recurrent wires
connect longtime with shorttime
devotions, doubt about yourself
hand over your earnings, pour down
mixtures of poison (do this as an early routine)
and get drunk of dawn, before daytime
when only the angry still can

from: *Copycat* (Prometheus 1996)

IN THE LABORATORY OF LOVE

estranged by the abbreviation
('please do not forget that funny, little thing')
I looked at her: mademoiselle mosquito
a bite on her vanilla coloured skin
before I did surrender to the changes of appearance
the boiling of the blood, the shiverings of our mood
and later listening to the sounds of two deterrent bodies
in cold and foamless water. Steam became dew, heat
became ice, and flesh became stone
bewildered, stirred, confused
we cut the barbed wire around our hearts
and waited for the days that followed
we felt as during chemistry lessons
curious to see what would be left
of what's left

from: *Obiit in orbit* (De Bezige Bij, 1999)

SOLARIS SOLITARIS

there is no reason for illusions
but still we want to believe

that life is worthy. We demand more
than we can find. All the rest

remains ideal - even for
whoever lives in wilderness

only seldom she is found
and always she is lost

in brightness. The place
of individuals remains their

solitude, solaris
solitaris

head bursting out of its skull
brain bursting out of its hulster
my ego has again departed
I is no longer the other
but a multitude of me

unriddle the structures of time
externalise your fears
befriend your neurosis

make sure heaven will lose
its utter sanctity

---

from: *Bloedtest* (De Bezige Bij, 2003)

ACE DRIVER (SENNA, † 1-5-1994)

I read about a man
who shot at his screen
when he learnt of your death
now you live here
in this gambling machine
your body turned into
a restless lead ball
a flickering name
A notice has been tacked to the wall
with drawing pins:

SVP: LIMITED PLAYING TIME
REF. OTHER PLAYERS

apt, don't you agree

Do you know, I wonder
what actually went through
that helmeted head of yours
when you took off
did you see magnificent fish
(rock-bass and bream)
gasping for air
or birds (minstrels, leadbeaks,
finches or linnets) with
crippled wings or naked,
pugilistic women?
Did you hear Beethoven blare
in your ear? An oratorio choir,
a last note, a deep bell
or precisely as here
the senseless soundtrack

of hell? It makes me wonder,
now that I can see your lights
flash amply again in front of me
now that I can hear the screeching
of your car in the last turn, no
the one before...

from: *Copycat* (Prometheus, 1999)

PSYCHOPATHIA SEXUALIS

Thus he imagines that he
steps into her dream; the house
of an acquaintance, a patient
a knock on the door, a small
tap on her head, a smile

he puts his leather bag
next to her bed, smells her
perfume (Bardot, or Givenchy)
the breath of eveningcoffee, but
not the slightest shade of fear

while he looks in his bag she asks
whether he'd like the window to be
opened, air and light to enter, but
he says he'd prefer not. He says
the room will anyway remain too small

she asks politely whether she
should undress. He nods and
takes on her clothes. He folds them
and puts them on the blanket; he helps her nice-
and orderly, because no passion must arise

he puts some drops of fluid in her
inflamed eyes, sprays haze
into her nose, cleans thoroughly
both lungs, puts his stethos
at her shoulderblades

and imagines how he opens up her
bottom with his nails, skins

her back and caresses her spine
(he thinks of laketrout, truite
à la meunière) and with his hands

he grabs at her veins that
curl around his fingers
he grasps at her heart that,
before he multiplies and cuts it
is being smothered by a kiss

a kiss! that age-old art
of self-restraint

from: *Copycat* (Prometheus, 1996)

THE CRASH

everything you knew
has vanished now

one push on a button
Delete/SysRq

you who thought it would be
nothing but a torn page

a blind spot in your memory
morris

something that would perish with age
or that would come by night

pale as the moon, as the scary face
of a screaming baboon

as a bony-white segment
an old wrinkled serpent

or as a night that would be
without end

but clearly it came on a blue
and bright day. Without delay

but directly in the sun
with a bang, blood and shredder

while asked around you were the only one
who knew the right word for the top

of a coffin: eternal look-out
wisecrack! In the wreckage

you proved that you could do without
while firemen were burning holes

in the roof-top you kept your eyes straight
at the sun

I do remember now, in fact
how death was called that day:

a cataract

from: *Obiit in orbit* (De Bezige Bij, 1999)

NIGHT IN HOTEL ORBIT

What you will find here in this resort
is a good and pleasant atmosphere'
the manager says. 'That's why we've called it
Hotel Orbit. It's English and easy for the ear
and good as such for customs sake'

in the rooms upstairs you find frayed nettings
a tv with sixteen channels mostly showing noise
a central VCR down at the reception desk
is playing movies filled with fragments
out of children's lives; the porno
is preferably consumed with paper cans
filled with icy pop or fresh, hot popcorn
coming out of the machines that are restlessly
zooming in the blue-carpeted hallways

on the toilet of the lobby one can find left-overs
grains of hash, a slogan that is burnt by smoker's ash
into the stained and orange colored doors:
'please don't let me die in this century'
and other words of poetry

you always wanted to be kidnapped
you always wanted to crawl on a floor
where your blood could not go
you were willing to take scourges
not knowing how they usually feel
you were willing to take pain
assuming that your body would heel

wounds always reminded you of flowers
desire of the things that are gone
and the things that you're still yearning for

are you longing to return to yourself?
are you willing to give up your soul?
are you longing for a room in this hotel?
where the walls are feeding on the fumes of visitors
where each body catches rheum, where each head
is going low, where each heart is being emptied
and each life is going slow

in this hotel nobody knows at breakfast time
what date it is, and what the number is
of the room that was assigned
in the afternoon one hears the shootings
outside, the echoes of the drums
soldiers' marching songs, the army
of our fate approaching at close range

cold-blooded, cool-headed, determined
these men of arms have plotted their attack
no settlement can be arranged
one sees our waiters carrying guns
serving on the very few remaining guests
outside who still enjoy the sun

checking out of this forgotten place
is not a matter hereof privacy
or one's own will; no one is free
to go back home. what as a little
summertrip began is destined to go on
how long ago since you arrived in this hotel
how many of your loved ones have already
died; do you feel sorrow or remorse
for the persons you have loved the most?
are you happy with the atmosphere?

can you tell lucidity from fear?
no panic, be secure, be calm
the oxygen is almost gone
fresh air is running thin

was it cancer or old age your parents
perished by, who drove the car
that killed your dearest friend
and in whose hands would you prefer
to put your trust mistakenly
in here your one and only company
is solitude, in here one says
you should be grateful you're alone

nobody is allowed to receive visitors
nobody likes to be disturbed
this is – of course –
'to your greater security'
and the comfort of us all
thus are the rules set by the personnel
and such is the nature of this weary crew

this is the place where very soon
you will be one of those persons
missing, this is the place where
very soon you will be one of those
reported dead or disappeared

the world outside will never understand
what happened in fact nobody
will ever know
nor will they care

whether you still exist (or not)
or ever were alive
you realize that what you are
was merely in your blood

and now quite sharply things appear
and everything seems clear

from: *Obiit in orbit* (De Bezige Bij, 1999)

NYCTALOPE

Your face is never bright
You always seek the dark
Part of your face has disappeared
You say that you are through
with this world, Christ -
you could die like a deer
here in this room
antlers drilled into a cortex
a hole in the skull
ice behind the eyes -
but no one
wanted it like that
Is this another new disease
or a symptom of love
in a sick room?
the alarm clock says it for you:
tomorrow you will wake up
newly born

from: *The Palace of Sleep* (Prometheus, 1993)

NOTES ON CONTRIBUTORS

Adam Gaucher was born Adam Gosha (pronounced go-shay) in Rochester, MN on 11 December 1982. He began writing around the age of 15, and has since compiled many collections of works, including: "Verbatim in Ground Beef," and, "Dancing Against Sanity and Winning the Prize." In 2001 he graduated from the Studio Academy High School for the Arts, and is now set on a future in Toronto, Canada. Visit the poet at http://members.aol.com/jasterdan/

Alexander Shaumyan was born in Moscow, Russia, in 1962 and immigrated to the United States in 1975 at the age of 13. He started out as a painter but turned to poetry as a more effective medium for expressing his message. His work appeared in many small presses and online journals. He's also done translations of Russian, German, French, Spanish, and Italian poetry. His translation of Nikolai Gumilev has been published online. His translation of Sergey Esenin's last poem appeared in *Glas,* Volume 23—the internationally known journal of new Russian writing, edited by Natasha Perova. His poetry has been taught by Professor Gerald Smith at Oxford University, who teaches modern Russian poetry and émigré Russian literature. In 2002 he published three books of poetry: "Spirit of Rebellion", "Canzoni dimenticate" and "Through the Eyes of Love". He published his fourth book of poetry "Place Where Light Is" in July, 2003. He graduated with a Bachelor's degree in psychology from Southern Connecticut State University in 1985. In 1998 he received a Master's degree in mathematics from Eastern Kentucky University. He's currently a part-time instructor in mathematics at Southern Connecticut State University, while pursuing his underground life of a dissident émigré

Russian poet. His biographical profile will appear in *Who's Who in America*, 2004, published by Marquis Who's Who (http://www.marquiswhoswho.com) scheduled to be published in November, 2003.

Christine Kempster is from Herts, Great Britain. "My name is Christine and until the new millennium I was happy being a wife and mother, building a home and very little more. There was a knock on the door one day and that's when things began to happen. I went to a creative writing workshop and discovered I could write poetry, I went to college and learned how to use my computer professionally, which led to three teaching certificates, now I teach adults how to use a computer and occasionally hold poetry workshops of my own. I have suffered two tragic losses over the last six months but in themselves they have made me stronger and now I do not look back but forward to a glorious future filled with poetry, friends, family and teaching. I may be 52 years old but I have a lifetime of living ahead of me."

Colette "I have been writing poetry and creating art since I was a little girl. This imaginative vein, as a child, was perhaps utilized as a form of escapism. I view the art that I pen, paint and mould, as an adult, as key ingredients for my healing life recipe.I am a survivor of failed relationships, leukemia, and numerous complications that were the result of a bone marrow transplant. Through it all, hope has carried me to the realization of improved health, and the dream of reciprocated love. I'm in love with LIFE. I'm in love with NATURE. I'm in love with LOVE. I'm infatuated by the story of Cupid & Psyche. Often, I make comparisons of myself to Psyche in my poetry. I have written my own version of this romantic tale, my reality, which is a relentless pursuit for love. Along with Psyche, who acquired butterfly wings, I am enamored by the transformation of butterflies. I work with butterflies from their chrysalis stage forward, flowers and weeds. From all, I see determination for survival, and inspiration for my art, poetry and life. The predominant theme in my poetry is LOVE...the longing I have for it, and the sense of loss I've experienced with it. Though is may be clear what my subject matter is, I adore playing with metaphors, and often weave multiple meanings within each poem. I have written my autobiography "Smiling through the Tears," and intend on seeking an agent soon. It's my desire to get my life story published in the big league, and yes, onto the big screen too! I believe it will relay a powerful message of HOPE to all. Currently, I am a student at Kendall College of Art & Design in Grand Rapids, Michigan, where I'm studying Fine Arts with emphasis on painting. Like my poetry, my art is raw with emotion. If you would be interested in viewing my art, reading more of my poetry, would like to learn more about me, or want to email me some of your poetry to post on my website, please visit me at www.POETDREAMS.com."

Daniel W. Gonzales is a writer in Whittier, California. A career college student who has been in the process of studying English Literature for seven years on and off but has finally made a commitment to his major and vows to earn a degree in Creative Writing so that he may become a teacher of it. In 2000, he lost his grandfather, Robert F. Shorb, then in 2002, he lost his grandmother, Helen P. Shorb and now this year on June 3rd, 2003, he lost his mother, Beverly K. Gonzales. Death seems to follow Danny wherever he goes but he has decided not to be bitter but to confront his grief and make the most of his short time here on earth.

Danielle Ackley-McPhail began devouring books at a very young age and eventually developed the talent for telling tales of her own. This love of the written word has followed her throughout her life. She has shared her time and talent with various literary publications, including *The Cantilever*; the literary journal of Florida Southern College; *The Grubstreet Writer*, the literary journal of Kean College of NJ; *The Taj Mahal Review*, published by Cyberwit; and *The Amazing Instant Novelist*, an on-line writing area sponsored by America Online. Her work has also appeared in the November 2002 and February 2003 issues of *Sabledrake Magazine* (www.sabledrake.com) and is included in the anthologies *Through a Glass Darkly* (released by Lite Circle Publications) and both *Passion*, and *Voyages - An Anthology of World Poetry* published by Cyberwit. Her current ongoing project is a bi-monthly writer's column entitled *If We'd Words Enough and Time*, for the internet Literary site, Fictionauts.com. With Bachelors Degrees in both English and Communications from Kean College of NJ, she has worked in the publishing industry for the past nine years. She is currently employed as a Production Manager for Random House. With this, her first novel, she explores the rich mythology of her Celtic heritage and her own longtime fascination with fantasy. At the turn of the New Year, she completed the sequel, *Tomorrow's Memories*, which is currently under consideration by a major publishing house. Danielle lives in New York with her husband, Mike, mother-in-law Teresa, and two extremely spoiled cats.

Darla Elaine Fitzgerald is a retired elementary teacher from Marshall County, West Virginia. Through her poetry, she hopes to instill inspirational thinking and touch emotional consciousness of readers. Her poetry has been published on Write-Away! and Harvest-Art. Darla resides in Ohio with her husband, Bill. They have 5 adorable grandchildren. Her poetry has been accepted for publication with online and printed magazines. Online: *Word Salad, Write-Away!, Firstwriter, Electric Acorn, Wellspring Journal*, *Spirit in the Smokies,* and *Poetic Voices* Printed: *Poet's Paradise, Eve's Back, Poetic Hours, Promise, Carillon, Rearview Quarterly, Reflections*, *New Renaissance, Write On!!, Natural Awakenings, Taj Mahal Review, Voyages, FreeXpresSion*, and *Terrace Journal.*

Del Senkbeil, a retired secretary with 500 poems copyrighted on different websites, lives in Sheboygan, Wisconsin, a city of approximately 50,000 located on the shores of beautiful Lake Michigan. "I have been expressing my thoughts and feelings in poetry since I was in grade school. I also collect coins and vintage sheet music. For over three years now writing poetry for poetry sites on the internet has been my pride and joy."

Dr Henry Victor, professor, priest, and poet, is originally from Sri Lanka with roots in South India from where he also obtained his initial degrees before he went to United Kingdom for his doctoral studies in Islamics. He, with his wife and their only daughter Gitanjali, now has migrated to Canada. Dr Henry Victor was formerly a Senior Lecturer in Comparative Religion and Head of Department of Islamic Studies in the Eastern University, Sri Lanka. He had been also a Visiting Lecturer in number of Theological Institutes in Sri Lanka, India, and United Kingdom. He is at present a Research Fellow at the Milan V. Dimic Research Institute and a Visiting Professor at the Department of Comparative Literature, Religion, and Film/Media Studies of the University of Alberta and an Anglican Priest of the Diocese of Edmonton. Dr Henry Victor has written several research articles for academic journals published in Sri Lanka, India and United Kingdom. He has participated and presented papers in numerous national and international conferences. Earlier Henry Victor's poems were published in two collections titled **No Tears** (1998) and **Frail Floret** (1999). Many of his poems have also appeared in numerous magazines, journals, and anthologies published from Sri Lanka, India, Philippines, Germany, United Kingdom, United States, and Canada. Some of his poems have been translated into German and Tamil languages as well. Henry Victor's poems won three awards in the Edmonton (Alberta) Song of the Street Poetry Competition the year 2002. Some years ago a collection of Victor's poems titled "Poems on War and Peace", published by the University of Uppsala, Sweden was banned by the then Sri Lankan Government. A review of Henry Victor's **No Tears** reads: "The anguish of the war torn earth is genuinely portrayed directly … or more subtly suggested … has the vibration of some of the poetry of revolt …" Dr Henry Victor is an Anglican Priest of the Diocese of Edmonton committed to promoting inter-religious harmony and peace.

Herbert L. Burd resides in Acton, CA, USA working for the Walt Disney Studios in Burbank CA. His hobbies are writing poetry and researching his Cherokee heritage. "I have been writing ever since I was very young. Now at 49 years of age now I find that writing is such a beautiful gift. One that is given to be shared. Writing is such a release, an art to be able to paint with words. One day I may add music to my words just for the fun of it. I am German, English, Irish and Cherokee decent. I have chosen the road of the Cherokee. Many of my poems are romanticizing Native America. My goals are hard but then again any goal worth while is hard.

Trying to become a known poet and be able to make a living at it could be one of the hardest. But this is my choice"

Janet Buck from OR, USA is a six-time **Pushcart Nominee**. Her poetry has recently appeared in **CrossConnect, Poetry Magazine.com, The Montserrat Review, Offcourse, The Pedestal Magazine, Runes, Southern Ocean Review, PoetryBay, Tryst, The Rose & Thorn, Red River Review, Coelacanth, Facets Magazine**, and hundreds of journals worldwide. Janet's second print collection, **Tickets to a Closing Play**, was the winner of the **2002 Gival Press Poetry Award**; the book is scheduled for print publication in October of 2003. Buck's work is forthcoming in **Zuzu's Petals, The Pittsburgh Quarterly**, and **The Kenwood Review**. Visit the poet at http://members.aol.com/jbuck22874/whatsnew.htmland http://www.janetbuck.com

John Dempsey was born in Cairo, Egypt and came to the United States in 1980 where he set up residence in Greenwich Village, New York. Mr. Dempsey currently makes a living as a technical consultant for various businesses in Manhattan as well as free lance writing assignments. 'Steps to the Madhouse', John's first collection of work, is currently available as an E-book, through Brainpan Publishing), and is enjoying favorable reviews. (http://brainpanpublishing.0catch.com/bookstore/bookstore.htm)

Presently Mr. Dempsey is working with Irishwrite Publishing on his second collection of work and the tentative release date has been set for July of 2003. (http://www.iriswhite.com/index.html) Personal Website: http://www.geocities.com/jdempseysbox/intro.html

Prof. Dr. Kazuyosi Ikeda has greatly contributed to science as professor of theoretical physics, publishing over 100 scientific papers and 10 scientific books. Currently he is professor emeritus of Osaka University, President of International Earth Environment University, Senator and Plenipotentiary Minister for Japan of International Parliament for Safety and Peace, Senator and Plenipotentiary Minister for Asian States of the Council of the

States for Protection of Life, Deputy Director General of International Biographical Centre (in UK), Deputy Governor of American Biographical Institute, and responsible officer of many other world-famous organizations. Ph.D. of Science (from Japan), Hon. Doctor of Science (from Germany), Hon. Doctor of Literature (from UK, Germany, Australia), Cultural Doctorate in Poetical Literature (from USA), Hon. Doctor of Environmental Science (from USA). As a distinguished poet, he published innumerable poems in Japanese and English in the 7 and 5 syllable metre (sitigotyo : Japanese traditional beautiful metre) mainly on the hearts of many things, based on his philosophy that all creations have hearts as God's gifts, with the aim of establishment of universal brotherhood and world peace. He also makes haiku, tanka and Chinese fixed-form classical poetry originated in the Tang perriod. He published 27 literary books (including 15 collections of poems), and over 50 literary essays and articles. His biography is included and featured in about 50 international famous Who's Who books in the world. Conferred on him, were Yukawa Scholarship Award, International Order of Merit, Chevalier Grand Cross, Golden Academy Award for Lifetime Achivement, the 20th centure Achievement Award, the 21st Century Achievement Award, International Honours Cup, Albert Einstein Academy Award for Outstanding Achievement, Order of Pegasus of Highest Degree, International Commendation of Success in Physics and Literature, Outstanding Professional Award in Science and Literature, N.S. Chandra bose National Award for Excellence in Poetry and Environmental Science, the titles of Grand Ambassador of Achievement, World Laureate, Knight of the Templar order, Knight of the Holy Grail Order, Knight of the Lofsensic Ursenius Order, Knight of the Universal Knights Order, Knight Commander of the Sovereign Order, Most Influential Scientist, Best World Poet, Outstanding Man of the 20th Century, Outstanding Man of the 21st Century, Poet of the Mellennium, and innumerable other honours and prizes.

Richard Conrad Henry was born in Turin, Italy in '64. Moved to Holland in '81. Started writing in '85. He has been published by Skyline Publishings (in their Feb. issue 2002) and Shadow Poetry included him in their collection (Dec. 2002). His work is also featured on several 'on-line' poetry sites, www.Rosedog.com, www.Authorsden.com to name a few.

Serge van Duijnhoven (born 1970 in Oss, in the south of the Netherlands) is a performing poet, novelist, playwright and art-editor. He is the author of several books of fiction and non-fiction. Among them four books of poems: *The Palace of Sleep* (1993), *Copycat* (1996), *End of the Line: Phantom City* (1997), *Obiit in Orbit; at the other end of the night* (1999). All of these books are published in Dutch, by recognized publishing houses. In the last two books cd's are included. Since 1995 the author performs his poetry with electronic music and video-projections in his literary band 'Dichters Dansen Niet' (Poets Don't Dance), together with DJ Fat and VJ Gabriel Kousbroek. In 2003 a new collection of poems with a cd from the band Poets Don't Dance will appear: *Bloedtest* (*Bloodtest*). Van Duijnhoven also wrote two books of prose: *Poets don't dance* (1995) and *The Other Side & Happiness* (1995), as well as a minibiography on the late emperor of Ethiopia *Haile Selassie* (1993), and a monologue for theatre *Songs of Vranje* (2000) that was published at TeleXpress and played throughout the Rotterdam Cultural Capital of Europe 2001 events at Las Palmas. He was the winner of the Nova Makedonia Poetry Award at the Poetry Festival of Struga 1995, and the Initiator of MillenniuM; the periodical 'timebook' of the Art Group of the Lowlands. For the occasion of the Struga Poetry Evenings, Serge's poetry was translated into Macedonian by Suzana Dapcevka, and published by Detska Radost (Palatata da sonot, 1995). In the fall of 1999 his book *We call them Roses* was published, a collection of personal impressions gathered during five years of travelling through the Balkan region. The book reached the longlist of the 'Gouden Uil Literatuurprijs 2000' (Golden Owl Literature Price of Flanders). Photographers in Wartime (2002), a book with an extended essay and stirring photos from reknown 'eyes of the war' like Nachtwey, Tim Page a.o., appeared in 2002 both in English and Dutch within the Ludion-Beaux Arts collection in cooperation with the Flanders Fields World War I Museum in Ieper. Serge's latest book is called Bloodtest (De Bezige Bij, 2003) - published together with a cd from his band 'Poets Don't Dance'. In the summer of 2000 he participated in the Literaturexpress; a train with about one hundred European writers on board, representing fourtythree European countries. The train was an initiative of the LiteraturWERKstatt Berlin:

it crossed Europe from Lisbon through Brussels all the way to Moscow, and then back through Minsk and Warshaw to the final stop: Berlin. Coming year his novel *Boulevard Oktoberrevolution* will appear, a book set in an unspecified beleaguered city 'somewhere far away in Europe'. In 1995, Serge lived for a while in Sarajevo. Before that, he lived in Amsterdam (the Netherlands), Luverne Minnesota (USA) and France. Currently he lives in Brussels, Belgium, where he is working as a freelance reporter, especially on Balcan matters, for Dutch and Flemish media. Visit his own website at www.sergevanduijnhoven.com with fragments in Real Audio and texts in four languages (Dutch, English, German and French).